If David Shibley had been born
in every "History's Missionary Heroes book today. That's why we
need to listen to him now—he's a voice to our generation for effective
missionary enterprise as history is being made today. His timely book
Living as if Heaven Matters will stir your heart to invest your life for
those things which are ultimately important.

—Jack W. Hayford
Chancellor, The King's College and Seminary

This communiqué is to express my endorsement of Dr. David Shibley's
book *Living as if Heaven Matters*. His father and mother were cofounders
of the Osborn Foundation in 1949. I have known David since he was
a Bible-quoting lad. This book will mark this generation. David is a
witness of Jesus Christ. He is a committed messenger to the world,
profoundly influencing pastors and Christian leaders with God's dream
of telling people about His Son, Jesus. His passion is to share Christ.
His field is the nations of the world. He believes that to be a Christian is
to be universal; that Jesus is the face of God; that Christianity is Christ;
that Christians are people who believe in God and humanity and *life*
through Christ. He believes we would never have known what God
is like if we had not looked into the face of Jesus. Seeing His love in
action stirs us to be like Him, to live for what matters forever. To hear
His "Well done!" *is* real success. Read this and sense God's passion, hear
His voice, and discover yourself in His plan.

—T. L. Osborn
Author, *Healing the Sick*
Founder, Osborn Ministries International

A book like this is long overdue. Every Christian should read this book.
The "me" generation has had its day and taken its toll. This book will
help people to focus on what matters most. Highly recommended.

—R. T. Kendall
Author, *Total Forgiveness*

However this book happened into your hands, I can assure you that
you're about to encounter a life-enriching experience. It is, in my
opinion, a must-read for every believer who wonders what God is

trying to say to a troubled church in an age of misguided priorities. *Living as if Heaven Matters* has brought back into focus what really matters in life—living for Jesus with an eye on eternity. It has filled my heart with a renewed anticipation of the joys of heaven and the hope of eternity that awaits every follower of Jesus Christ.

—Dick Eastman
President, Every Home for Christ

The apostle Peter told us at the close of his life that he expected an *abundant* entrance into the everlasting kingdom (2 Pet. 1:11). If that is true, it must be possible to stand in heaven at the judgment seat of Christ having a *meager* entrance. As Christians, none of us want to "just make it in." I believe it is essential we learn about that great event so we will not be unprepared. Dr. David Shibley has done a great work in making that day clear and understandable in his book *Living as if Heaven Matters.* It is a privilege to recommend to you this book that has greatly impacted me.

—Bob Yandian
Senior Pastor, Grace Church, Tulsa, OK

There is no doubt that God has put eternity into the hearts of men. The Bible states it as fact…as the Word of God. My extensive work with men has allowed me to see the distractions that most men have that puts this view of heaven in a compartmentalized place we seldom enter. But when we do, God stirs our hearts for home…and Him. David Shibley is one of the most compelling advocates in our lifetime for turning our hearts toward home. His influence around the world as a statesman of the highest regard for the kingdom of God is well known. This book will give insight into the reason for his passion—that every man, woman, and child on the planet know about the soon-coming appointment with eternity, reward, and giving account for our lives. I heartily recommend this work to the men and women who are living for His highest!

—Rick Kingham
President, The Center for Global Mobilization
President, National Coalition of Men's Ministries

LIVING
as if
HEAVEN
MATTERS

DAVID SHIBLEY

Charisma
HOUSE
A STRANG COMPANY

Most Strang Communications/Charisma House/Siloam/FrontLine/Realms products are available at special quantity discounts for bulk purchase for sales promotions, premiums, fund-raising, and educational needs. For details, write Strang Communications/Charisma House/Siloam/FrontLine/Realms, 600 Rinehart Road, Lake Mary, Florida 32746, or telephone (407) 333-0600.

Living as if Heaven Matters by David Shibley
Published by Charisma House
A Strang Company
600 Rinehart Road
Lake Mary, Florida 32746
www.charismahouse.com

Scripture quotations marked PHILLIPS are from *The New Testament in Modern English*, Revised Edition. Copyright © 1958, 1960, 1972 by J. B. Phillips. Macmillan Publishing Co. Used by permission.

Scripture quotations marked THE MESSAGE are from *The Message: The Bible in Contemporary English*, copyright © 1993, 1994, 1995, 1996, 2000, 2001, 2002. Used by permission of NavPress Publishing Group.

Cover design by John Hamilton Design (www.johnhamiltondesign.com)
Executive Design Director: Bill Johnson

Library of Congress Cataloging-in-Publication Data

Shibley, David.
  Living as if heaven matters / David Shibley. -- 1st ed.
    p. cm.
  Includes bibliographical references and index.
  ISBN 978-1-59979-166-1 (trade paper)
  1. Christian life. 2. Future life--Christianity. 3. Heaven--Christianity. I. Title.
  BV4501.3.S547 2007
  248.4--dc22

                                          2007020222

First Edition

07 08 09 10 11 — 9 8 7 6 5 4 3 2 1
Printed in the United States of America

To my parents:

Lillian Shibley, living with us in Texas,

and

Warren Shibley, living with Jesus in heaven.

They taught me to seek another world.

ACKNOWLEDGMENTS

I AM GRATEFUL FOR LONG-STANDING FRIENDSHIPS WITH SEVERAL people at Strang Communications. Stephen Strang has been a friend and personal encourager for more than twenty years. *TIME* magazine has rightly acknowledged his impact and ever-growing influence for the cause of Christ. I'm especially appreciative for the very capable editorial team at Charisma House: Barbara Dycus, Deborah Moss, and Jevon Bolden. It was a joy to work with each of them.

God has given Global Advance a fantastic staff. It is an honor for me to lock arms with them to advance the Great Commission by equipping the church's hidden heroes in underserved regions of the world. Anna Holland, my excellent assistant, has been a great liaison between our office and the publisher. Our team has strengthened me throughout the process of seeing this book to completion.

Naomi and I are undergirded by a great group of friends who pray daily for us and the ministry in our stewardship. They literally prayed me into a new season of fruitfulness in writing. These "inner circle intercessors" are part of a host of people who make possible the ministry of Global Advance through their prayers and missions gifts. I extend my heartfelt thanks to each of our partners. Also, each year we meet with a few friends in ministry who provide friendship, pastoral counsel, and oversight. Special thanks to our co-workers in His harvest who comprise this group.

I'm deeply grateful for my partnership in the gospel with outstanding leaders of the church in many developing nations. Most of these men and women face persecution and threats because of their devotion to Christ. They truly live as if heaven matters.

I can't forget to thank three wonderful people: my parents, who built a home of love where Jesus was truly Lord, and Gertrude Nathan, the vacation Bible school teacher who shared the gospel and led me in opening my young heart to Jesus as my Savior and King. They pointed me toward the pilgrimage that leads to the celestial city.

Most of all I thank God for my precious wife, Naomi. Since our marriage in 1972 she has been supremely supportive of God's call on my life. She just keeps excelling—beautiful wife, fabulous mother, awesome grandmother, compassionate servant of Christ. Thank you for loving me and sharing life with me.

Now I saw a new heaven and a new earth, for the first heaven and the first earth had passed away. Also there was no more sea. Then I, John, saw the holy city, New Jerusalem, coming down out of heaven from God, prepared as a bride adorned for her husband. And I heard a loud voice from heaven saying, "Behold, the tabernacle of God is with men, and He will dwell with them, and they shall be His people. God Himself will be with them and be their God. And God will wipe away every tear from their eyes; there shall be no more death, nor sorrow, nor crying. There shall be no more pain, for the former things are passed away." Then He who sat on the throne said, "Behold, I make all things new."

—Revelation 21:1–5

CONTENTS

Introduction 1

1 Anchored Upward 5

2 A Rich Welcome 19

3 You Can Only Imagine 29

4 Heaven: The Safest Investment on Earth 41

5 By His Wounds 53

6 Death's Demise 61

7 The Chemistry of the Universe 73

8 Is That Your Final Answer? 83

9 Vindicated at Last! 97

10 A Sure Reward 109

11 Treasures in Heaven 119

12 Built to Last 135

13 Seeing the Invisible 147

14 A Theology of Hope 163

Scripture Index 183

Notes 189

INTRODUCTION

Y OUR MOST IMPORTANT APPOINTMENT EVER IS NOT FAR OFF.
You have a scheduled, personal appointment with Jesus
Christ—and you will keep this appointment.

But how do you prepare? That is the subject of this book. You can
live today—and every day—for what matters forever. You can live in
heaven's honor.

For too long we have preached and lived a pseudogospel that
suggested every person could do what seemed right in his own eyes.
And we've reaped the bitter fruit. A deadening nihilism is choking much
of contemporary culture. A glut of media assaults us from all directions.
Boredom and fatigue have gripped even the young. Many have fallen
prey to what Stuart McAllister calls "an entertainment-blinded life of
perpetual distraction and seduction."[1]

The church has by no means escaped this onslaught. Much of the
church has both swallowed and been swallowed by forms of existen-
tialism. The emphasis has been on *now* and *me*. But recently, amid the
agony of our self-inflicted wounds, God has been lovingly wooing us
back to accountability—to Him and to each other. With the advent
of the new millennium, and especially after 9/11, the pendulum began
to swing back toward an eternal orientation. For the first time in a
long time people are talking again about being "homesick for heaven."
The tremendous reception some years ago to MercyMe's song "I Can

1

Only Imagine" signals a return to a widespread longing for our eternal home.

For such healthy readjustment to continue we must have a new perception of things. This new focus calls for some new definitions, particularly regarding what constitutes true success in life. Dietrich Bonhoeffer, who died in a Nazi prison camp, said, "The figure of the Crucified invalidates all thought which takes success for its standard."[2] Prayerfully we are entering a season when the standard is not success (as it has been popularly defined) but obedience. Pleasing Jesus is the bottom line. We live as if heaven matters when we live to hear Christ's "well done" over our lives.

New goals, then, are in order. Our hearts' desires must come into line with His. Living in light of our sure appointment with Him brings a new set of drives; the only accolade that really matters is His. This releases the eternity-driven Christian to incredible freedom and joy now, in this life. "Aim at Heaven and you will get Earth 'thrown in,'" wrote C. S. Lewis. "Aim at Earth and you will get neither."[3]

The thrust of this book is to pull us back to the historic emphasis the Christian faith has always given to heaven and its rewards. *The big deal in this life is preparing for the big event in the afterlife*—when we give an account of our stewardship to none other than Jesus Himself. Because of our colossal neglect of this area in recent years, a list of all Bible verses referenced is provided for your further study. It's high time we understand from Scripture what it means to live in light of eternity, in honor of heaven.

I could never properly acknowledge all the friends, teachers, and co-workers in ministry who have helped me have a heart turned toward heaven. But I do express my indebtedness to each one. I'm grateful to Stephen Strang and the excellent team at Strang Communications for helping craft this book. It was a joy to work with Barbara Dycus, a truly outstanding editor, and her skilled editorial team. As always, I'm so grateful for Naomi, my precious wife, and her unwavering support. We prayed often over the developing manuscript. Naomi read every word and provided very helpful insights, suggestions, and encouragement.

Many years ago Henry Ward Beecher, a noted preacher of his day, expressed his yearning for eternity. "I have drunk at many a fountain but thirst came again. I have fed at many a bounteous table but hunger returned. I have seen many bright and beautiful things but while I gazed their luster faded. There is nothing here that can give me rest; but when I behold Thee, O God, I shall be satisfied!" The heart's eternal longings can be met only by what is eternal.

Soon we will stand before Jesus to give an account of our stewardship and receive any rewards we may have won. May Jude's benediction to his readers grace your heart as you read these pages and prepare for that day: "Now to Him who is able to keep you from stumbling, and to present you faultless before the presence of His glory with exceeding joy, to God our Savior, who alone is wise, be glory and majesty, dominion and power, both now and forever. Amen" (Jude 24).

CHAPTER ONE

ANCHORED UPWARD

He has also set eternity in the hearts of men.

—ECCLESIASTES 3:11, NIV

Here is one of the most unquestionable notes of the true church: the uplifted gaze. The church of the New Testament is anchored upward, not downward; its drawing is forward, not backward.

—A. J. GORDON

IT WAS THE DAY THE WORLD CHANGED.

The unthinkable happened. No pyrotechnics from even the most gruesome horror movie had ever envisioned anything so ghastly. On September 11, 2001, we watched a new reality emerge, a much more fragile world. Terrorism on a broad scale doesn't just happen "over there." It is now a constant threat where we live, work, and play.

Americans were dumbfounded on that horrific day. How could these fanatics have committed such acts of barbarism? Why did they do it? What would possess them to execute this twenty-first-century version of a kamikaze raid?

The answer, if there is one, is complex. But one thing should be understood. Their motive was not merely political; it was theological. As hideous as it seems—and as hideous as it truly is—the terrorists' misguided beliefs falsely promised them an instant paradise and a sure reward. Most of the world perceives these terrorists as lunatics. Using any standards by which we judge civilized people, they are. But these wildly religious people were acting out of a belief system that seemed logical to them. Don't ever think your theology doesn't affect your actions.

A voice for justice begins to scream inside us, "Will anyone ever *pay* for this? Will these mass murderers *ever* be brought to any kind of account?" If you believe the Bible, the answer is an absolute yes.

Philip Yancey observes, "For a society unsure whether evil even exists, and embarrassed by the word *sin*, it takes an atrocity of historic dimensions to raise the question once again. Moral ambiguity tends to recede as the nightly news portrays the stark contrast between death and life, between murder and rescue, between those who joke in Afghan caves about their unexpected success and those who dig for bodies in the pile of twisted steel."[1]

Most Americans rightly denounce any acts of terrorism done in the name of the Almighty by any group as unspeakably perverse. Christians in particular know it is completely foreign to everything biblical Christianity stands for. As Christians we realize that if God needs any avenging, He is fully capable of undertaking it Himself. "'Vengeance is Mine, I will repay,' says the Lord" (Rom. 12:19). To perpetrate death and destruction in God's name is not an expression of His will; rather, it is an affront to His very nature.

Many terrorists have embraced a misguided passion that for their final act of "bravery" they will be ushered immediately into something of an unending harem. (What a shock awaits them.) For them, these sensual pleasures would be paradise. But for followers of Jesus Christ, the big payoff for us is not sensual pleasure. It is a "well done" from Jesus Himself.

Yet we dare not miss the deeper point in all of this. Although terrorists are totally misguided in their theology, they have taken a truth and twisted it into a dark falsehood. It is true; God will reward our deeds. It is completely untrue that God would ever reward such barbarous brutality. But deceived radicals throughout the world are willing to die not only for their beliefs but also for the hope of commendation and compensation in the afterlife. And this concept is *not* foreign to Christianity.

Here's another big lesson from 9/11. Everything we hold dear in this life we can only hold loosely. Life here on earth is tenuous and short. James calls it "a vapor."[2] But for followers of Jesus, we're comforted to know life doesn't end here. Life goes on—better life, eternal life. We are a people with an anchor on the 9/11s of life. We are anchored upward.

The Missing Factor

To those familiar with scriptural incentives, the prospect of spending eternity with the Lord and being rewarded by Him is one of life's highest motivations. That is, it should be. But until recently there has been a dearth of teaching about eternity. Nor have we been sufficiently alerted to the coming great accounting when we will stand before Jesus Christ.

Think about it. When was the last time you heard a pastor teach about heaven or hell? Eternity has taken a backseat to more "relevant" topics. Judson Cornwall observed:

> It has been many years since I have heard a Christian testify to homesickness for heaven, and even longer since I have heard a sermon extolling the joys of heaven. Perhaps it is because this generation has a heaven without substance. Their heaven has no reality; there is nothing that the soul can really reach out and take hold of. To them heaven is an ambiguous, nebulous nothing that is reputed to follow the death of the believer—and they're supposed to really enjoy it if they ever get there.[3]

This book is a call to see life in the unblinking light of eternity. It is a challenge to view genuine success not in terms of earthly acclaim or possessions, but rather in terms of a "well done" from Jesus. Terrorists and Christians both anticipate a payoff after they die. But while they are impelled by a false conception of a wrathful deity, we are motivated by a biblical understanding of a God of love: "For the love of Christ compels us" (2 Cor. 5:14). The prospect of eternal rewards, dispensed by Jesus Himself, is the call to ultimate success. To receive Christ's approval and accompanying rewards for a life of service for Him—this is worth more than a million worlds.

Charles F. Kettering said, "We should all be concerned about the future, because that is where most of us will be spending the rest of our lives."[4] Yet we are probably the most immediacy-oriented generation in history. Deferred gratification just doesn't compute with many today. The secularization of society has plagued the church as well. In fact, part of the reason for the famine of preaching about eternity is that, until recently, most people just weren't interested. Pastors want to be relevant and preach to felt needs. And few have been feeling the need for heaven or desire rewards that, in their minds, seem roughly equivalent to celestial versions of bowling trophies.

But if we scratch right below the surface, we find a gnawing yearning for more than the material. When we are yanked out of the mad pursuit for pleasure by the death of a friend or a life-altering accident, we realize again that we are meant for more than a daily lap in a rat race. Our sterile technology and rationalism have produced a thirst for metaphysical experience. Many attempt to quench this thirst with bizarre trips into forms of Eastern religions, a self-styled spirituality, or flirtations with the occult. But this deep inner thirst can only be satiated by coming to the One who two thousand years ago said, "If anyone thirsts, let him come to Me and drink" (John 7:37).

Many years ago E. M. Bounds sounded a prophetic warning that has been largely fulfilled in our day. "These are materialized and materializing times," he wrote. "Materialized times always exalt the earthly and degrade the heavenly. True Christianity always diminishes the earthly and augments the heavenly. If God's watchmen are not brave, diligent, and sleepless, Christianity will catch the contagion of the times and think little of and struggle less for heaven."[5]

EXISTENTIAL CHRISTIANITY

It is indicative of the times that a newer edition of a major evangelical denomination's hymnal deleted no fewer than seventeen hymns dealing with heaven and eternal rewards. Among these songs apparently considered obsolete, one heart-searching chorus asks:

> Must I go and empty-handed,
> Thus my dear Redeemer meet?
> Not one day of service give Him,
> Lay no trophy at His feet?[6]

Hymns about the "sweet by-and-by" have often been replaced with lusterless lyrics about the gritty present. Even the old songs we retain are often "contemporized" versions that delete references to rewards in heaven. In an increasingly hostile, volatile world, I hurt for Christians who attempt to "tough it out" with no concept of eternity. Much of our preaching has become essentially motivational homilies with a light Bible glaze on top. How sad to view trials, pressures, temptations, and reversals from a purely temporal perspective. One may be encouraged that the sun is going to come out tomorrow, as Annie sang, but what if it doesn't? What if things grow increasingly worse? What if, God forbid, some madman detonates a dirty bomb or a rogue nation launches a nuclear missile? Is faith then shipwrecked? It could be if we're not living in heaven's honor.

Let's get real. Things don't always add up down here. Good is not always compensated in kind. It will take another world for Christians who serve God and others in secret to be rewarded justly, fully, and openly.

Any brand of Christianity that is devoid of an eternal perspective is a stripped-down model and should be traded in for something sturdier. Frankly, if the message you're buying into infers that it's all about *now* and it's all about *you*, you've gotten a raw deal theologically. The Bible says, "If only for this life we have hope in Christ, we are to be pitied more than all men" (1 Cor. 15:19, NIV).

When this life is viewed as a mere blip on eternity's scale, the most rigorous trials can become "light afflictions" and prolonged agonies can be seen as "but for a moment." Paul was probably in the throes of intense personal pain, heartbreaking distress, and satanic attack when he wrote:

> For our light affliction, which is but for a moment, is working for us a far more exceeding and eternal weight of glory, while we do not look at the things which are seen, but at the things which are not seen. For the things which are seen are temporary, but the things which are not seen are eternal.
>
> —2 CORINTHIANS 4:17–18

It was this confidence in God's ultimate control that enabled Alexander Solzhenitsyn to find solace in the most nightmarish of circumstances. Speaking of his Gulag Archipelago experience under the fierce hand of communism, he reminisced, "I nourished my soul there, and I say without hesitation: *'Bless you prison,* for having been in my life.'"[7]

Ironically, it is not the positive pep talks but the assurance of eternal blessings with Christ that breeds superlative living in the midst of storms. So trade in that flimsy model of futureless faith for a biblical Christianity that won't depreciate. The barometer of blessing may not be "instant return on what you have sown," but that kind of "return" often evaporates anyway. Instead you will walk joyfully by faith, fully confident of a coming time when a just God will reward justly with no favoritism. The ministry of God's Spirit to you becomes your guarantee that even more wonderful things are ahead.

> Compared to what's coming, living conditions around here seem like a stopover in an unfurnished shack, and we're tired of it! We've been

given a glimpse of the real thing, our true home, our resurrection bodies! The Spirit of God whets our appetite by giving us a taste of what's ahead. He puts a little of heaven in our hearts so that we'll never settle for less.

—2 CORINTHIANS 5:3–4, THE MESSAGE

A pretty good gauge of spiritual health is to be ready at any moment to drop it all—no matter how great the earthly blessings—to be home with the Lord. In a word, it's just better. Like Paul, we recognize our responsibilities to family, friends, and to our callings. So we stay here until He restations us. But we don't buy into the lie; we're not duped into thinking that this life is the big deal. There's something more— more permanent, more thrilling, more fulfilling. "To depart and be with Christ…is *far better!*" (Phil. 1:23; emphasis added).

So That's This Ache

Recently I talked with a friend about writing this book. At first she seemed thoroughly disinterested in the subject. "What do I need with a book about heaven and rewards?" she asked. "I'm constantly on the run. Even if we take a vacation, it's a marathon of activities. My life is about soccer practices and meals from drive-up windows and advancing our careers, and you want me to think about *heaven?*"

But as I probed a little deeper her curiosity increased. "So that's this ache I've been feeling," she said. "I've had this inner longing for something, but I couldn't put my finger on what it was. I guess it's really a longing for heaven. I never thought about it because nobody's ever suggested to me that's what this longing is." And if we continue to search our souls, we discover that behind the longing for heaven is an innate longing for God Himself.

The Bible confirms this built-in longing for eternity:

For we know that when this earthly tent we live in is taken down— when we die and leave these bodies—we will have a home in heaven, an eternal body made for us by God himself and not by human hands. We grow weary in our present bodies, and we long for the day when we will put on our heavenly bodies like new clothing.

—2 CORINTHIANS 5:1–2, NLT

The very word for *man* or *human* in Greek means "upward looker." God has set eternity in our hearts. We are eternal beings; we are meant to be anchored upward. This life is merely an interim. And something deep inside us knows it.

We are poised to see a revolt of sorts against "relevant" teaching that is so drenched in the present that it is largely irrelevant to our deepest longings. And the heart's deepest longing, contrary to a lot of popular sermonizing, is not for wealth, "success," or "your destiny" (which almost always means your destiny *here*, not *there*). Our deepest yearning is for God Himself.

I realize this book is something of a voice crying in the wilderness. On the surface teaching on success in this life seems far more practical than a call to set our desires on another world. Yet, in the dark nights of the soul (and we all have them), we cry for a redefinition of relevancy. We look for something—anything—that *really lasts*.

CLOUDED THINKING ABOUT THE UNCLOUDED DAY

Augustine, the early church father, asked, "Why do we not know the country whose citizens we are? Because we have wandered so far away that we have forgotten about it."[8] There's a lot of misinformation out there about heaven. Yet Paul said our true citizenship is there.[9] Many seem to have a concept of heaven not far removed from that of Huck Finn, Mark Twain's fictional, mischievous boy. He viewed heaven as a place where people "go around all day long with a harp and sing, forever and ever."[10] But for biblically informed believers, the life after this one is the eternal continuation and intensifying of the new life that began when we committed our lives to Christ. On that day we were genuinely converted—not just our souls, but also our values. Things we previously pursued began to be unattractive, and things once disdained began to be embraced. When we surrender our lives to Jesus Christ, our motives and motivations begin to change. No longer is our passion merely to please ourselves. Now we long to please Jesus: "Therefore we make it our aim, whether present or absent, to be well pleasing to Him" (2 Cor. 5:9). Not content to just serve the Lord, we want to serve Him acceptably. We want to live in heaven's honor.

> Therefore, since we are receiving a kingdom which cannot be shaken, let us have grace, by which we may serve God acceptably with reverence and godly fear. For our God is a consuming fire.
> —HEBREWS 12:28–29

It's right belief (in Jesus Christ) that gets us into heaven. It's right behavior that qualifies us for eternal rewards. The Bible teaches that Christians will one day stand before the Lord, not recoiling in fear of possible expulsion but to receive His affirmation. There, at what the Bible terms the judgment seat of Christ, the Christian will be held accountable for his postconversion life; each action and motive will be weighed. This is both sobering and exciting. What you do today counts—forever. Charles Spurgeon, a great English preacher of the nineteenth century, said, "We should live each moment as though it were being recorded, for recorded it shall be."

Obviously such a prospect is a powerful prod to holy living since our selfish deeds will be exposed. But it is also a joyful expectation. It is before this *bema*—this judgment seat—that Jesus will reward good stewardship. To those who qualify by a life of service and surrender He will bestow honors that will outlast time.

It is little wonder that many Christians today are confused and disheartened. For if we view things from the perspective of this life only, it could sometimes appear that God is playing favorites. Some, who have labored faithfully with little appreciation, might be tempted to think

God is unjust, that He has forgotten His promises to relieve the weary and recompense the righteous.

But *if*, in fact, there is a day when cups of cold water secretly ministered in His name are openly honored, and *if* there is a grand event when the scales of justice are forever balanced, then the bleakest of pictures bursts with rays of hope. Surely this is at least part of what the Lord had in mind when He promised a day of radical power reversal when the meek will inherit the earth.[11] A. W. Tozer describes the meek person as the trusting believer who is "patient to wait for the day when everything will get its own price tag and real worth will come into its own. Then the righteous shall shine forth in the kingdom of their Father. He is willing to wait for that day."[12]

ONE HUNDRED YEARS FROM TODAY

Some avoid the subject of heaven because they have a subliminal fear of standing before God. But if we truly belong to Him through faith in His Son, there is nothing to fear. As the old hymn says, we will be "dressed in His righteousness alone, faultless to stand before the throne."[13]

Other Christians are concerned that a focus on heaven might diminish their commitment to advancing the kingdom of God here on Earth. They're concerned that heavenly minded Christians will just check out of any meaningful involvement in current issues of righteousness and justice. But if we view things from a proper biblical perspective this will never happen. In fact, a heart set on heaven will intensify your commitment to be an agent of change here on Earth. Dorothy Sayers wrote:

> It is precisely because of the eternity outside time that everything in time becomes valuable and important and meaningful. Therefore, Christianity...makes it of urgent importance that everything we do here should be rightly related to what we eternally are. "Eternal life" is the sole sanction for the values of this life.[14]

The future prospect for the person who has been born again is always bright. What do you, as a Christian, have to look forward to in heaven? In a word—*kindness*. This is part of the reason your ongoing life after death will be eternity-long. It will take that long for God to express the full scope of His love for you: "That in the ages to come He might show the exceeding riches of His grace in His kindness toward us in Christ Jesus" (Eph. 2:7). What a future!

So, where's your heart? Where's your focus?

> Since you have been raised to new life with Christ, set your sights on the realities of heaven, where Christ sits at God's right hand in the place of honor and power. Let heaven fill your thoughts. Do not think only about things down here on earth.
>
> —COLOSSIANS 3:1–2, NLT

Joseph Stowell, past president of Moody Bible Institute, observed:

> Heaven is primary. Heaven must become our first and ultimate point of reference. We are built for it, redeemed for it, and on our way to it. Success demands that we see and respond to *now* in light of *then*. All that we have, are, and accumulate must be seen as resources by which we influence and impact the world beyond. Even our tragedies are viewed as events that can bring eternal gain.[15]

Life's great issue, then, becomes living today for what matters forever, living in heaven's honor. What are you doing now that will be important one hundred years from today? If we prioritize in light of that question, we discover the abiding components are amazingly few. Very quickly the list whittles down to relationships.

One hundred years from today your present income will be inconsequential. One hundred years from now it won't matter if you got that big break, took the trip to Europe, or finally traded up to a Lexus. The cruel remarks made behind your back will be long since dead, as will be the people who made them. Whether you threw pizza dough for a living, threw strikeouts for a major league team, or threw your weight around in some corporate boardroom as a CEO just won't matter.

It will matter that you knew God. It will greatly matter, one hundred years from today, that you made a commitment of your life to Jesus Christ. It will matter what you said since every idle word will be brought into judgment.[16] It will matter what you did when you thought no one was looking, since every secret thing will be exposed.[17] It will be important that you loved your children (and others' children) and that you helped provide a base of emotional acceptance on which they built their lives. It will matter that you fit into God's purposes for your life and for your time.

Most people spend a minimum of forty hours each week investing in the present. Of course, this is both necessary and commendable. Honest labor is honorable. But these hours too can be invested for eternity. And while we spend vast amounts of time responding to the necessities of the passing present, wouldn't it be wise also to make some kind of preparation for forever?

Eternity and eternal rewards are the big deal. Twenty-two-year-old Jim Elliot understood that when he wrote in his journal, "That man is no fool who gives up that which he cannot keep to gain that which he cannot lose." Elliot would not live to his thirtieth birthday. Along with four other gallant missionaries, he was martyred in a bold attempt to get the gospel to the primitive Waodoni tribe. Elliot was driven by eternity and by the Great Commission. Today he is enjoying realities that have eternal value—what he cannot lose. And because he surrendered what he could not ultimately keep, many Waodoni are at this moment experiencing heaven along with him.

INTERSECTIONS WITH ETERNITY

We are trained to stuff the most experience possible into the shortest time frame possible. Perhaps one reason for this is the uncertainty so many feel in this terrorized new millennium. Shortly after the 9/11 attacks, the numbers of engagements and weddings soared. And around nine months later, there was a spike in the number of newborns. People saw the fragility of life and decided it was high time to get on with life.

This also may be part of the reason for this generation's mad pursuit of instant gratification. Teenagers, not at all sure that this planet will survive another decade, want to taste the full gamut of experiences "before it's too late." Hedonists preach that we should live only for today. Stores lure the already overextended with the most seductive bait—*you can have it now* with no payments until next year. A lifetime of character development is bartered for a single tryst of passion. We are a generation conditioned to sacrifice the eternal on the altar of the immediate.

Yet life's transcendent experiences beckon us back to ultimate realities. To be present at the birth of a child is to experience a miracle—the miracle of life. But even in this joyous celebration there's a little tap on the conscience—a reminder that this baby has not only begun to live, but this child has also begun to die.

Birth and death are transcendent experiences, times when Earth seems to interplay with eternity. But there's another birth, just as real and in some ways more real than physical birth. It is the spiritual new birth Jesus spoke of so often. And unless you experience this birth, you cannot experience true life here or hereafter. It is a trip back to ultimate roots for you to reverse the physical process to be born again spiritually. You go back to a childlike dependency on God alone ("becoming as little children"[18]) so you can then be reborn. Placing yourself fully in the hands of God, turning completely from any self-reliance to qualify you for heaven, you put your trust in the sacrifice of the One who died in your place, Jesus Christ. Then you enter a realm of transcendent spiritual reality you had never previously known.

Have you experienced this new birth? It is the only way to enter heaven and the eternal kingdom of God.[19] Heaven is indeed a cruel joke unless you come to know and love the Lord who reigns there. Perhaps some deep longing is being stirred in you even now as you read. An inner thirst, long suppressed, is suddenly crying out for living water.

Your thirst can be quenched. You can begin to live forever—starting now. Listen to this promise from the One who dispenses this water:

> Whoever drinks the water I give him will never thirst. Indeed, the water I give him will become in him a spring of water welling up to eternal life.
>
> —JOHN 4:14, NIV

Do you want this life-giving water? Do you desire this new birth? Then open up your life to Jesus Christ right now. Let Him cleanse you of all your past and pour His living water into your parched soul. Call out to Him. Go ahead, He's listening. Make this the prayer of your heart:

> *Lord Jesus, I want this living water. I want to be born again on the inside. Thank You for dying on the cross for me and paying for all my sins with Your blood. Right now, I turn away from my sins and my old life. I trust Your shed blood as the full payment for all my sins. I believe that You are the Son of God and that God has raised You from the dead. I now receive You as my own Savior and commit myself totally to You as my Lord. Thank You for hearing my prayer, forgiving my sins, and coming into my life as You promised.*

Did you sincerely pray that prayer? Then welcome to God's worldwide family! Welcome to a new dimension where life is now connected to eternity. You now belong to God. It's His promise: "But as many as received Him, to them He gave the right to become children of God, to those who believe in His name" (John 1:12).

For the follower of Jesus, life is an adventure of knowing God, walking with Him, and living for what matters forever. And at the end of life on this earth you can stand before Jesus accountable yet unafraid.

CHAPTER TWO

A RICH WELCOME

Be all the more eager to make your calling and election sure. For
if you do these things you will never fall, and you will receive a
rich welcome into the eternal kingdom of our Lord and Savior
Jesus Christ.

—2 PETER 1:10–11, NIV

If there is one word above another that will swing open the eternal
gates, it is the name of JESUS. There are a great many pass-words and
by-words down here, but that will be the countersign up above.[1]

—DWIGHT L. MOODY

ABOUT THIRTY YEARS AGO (WHEN I TOO WAS YOUNG), I MET A
young British pastor. We struck up an immediate friendship.
Since we lived on opposite sides of the Atlantic we seldom saw
each other, but we maintained contact through letters. (We lived then
in that ancient world before e-mail.)

I was saddened to hear some time back from his wife that he fought a
losing battle with cancer. He carried on his ministry in wrenching pain
and exhaustion. But his love for Christ and for people helped pump
spiritual adrenaline into his weakening body.

He wrote me concerning a series of messages he was preaching. Not
surprisingly, the subject was heaven. He wrote, "I've preached a timely

series on Christian behavior concluding with 2 Peter 1:11, 'an abundant entrance into heaven.' I believe we can enter heaven in different manners (though the sole way in is through Christ). So few seem to want this abundant entrance. Like Balaam, they wish to die the death of the righteous but are not prepared to live the life of the righteous."[2]

When we're faced with the acute prospect of stepping into eternity, heaven (and hell) appears more tangible. Indeed, the afterlife becomes as real (or more real) than this ephemeral stage. Shakespeare said, somewhat pessimistically, "All the world's a stage, and all the men and women merely players."[3] It is true that we are living out a drama that will be judged in the next world.

While many of today's TV preachers primarily emphasize God's blessings in the present, it was not always so. During the years of the Second World War in the 1940s things were different. The big-name evangelist of the time was Charles E. Fuller, and his *Old Fashioned Revival Hour* was broadcast live to millions worldwide on Sunday afternoons from the Municipal Auditorium in Long Beach, California. The audience filling that hall was often young American sailors awaiting orders to be sent to the watery battlefronts of the Pacific.

Fuller realized that for many of these young men, each broadcast could be their last chance to hear the gospel and respond to Jesus Christ. His heartfelt compassion reached out to those sailors, and hundreds committed their lives to Christ.

By the radio sets back home, anxious parents sat listening and praying that their sons were in attendance. And many grieving parents and newly widowed young women were also listening. They had recently lost their loved ones in battle. Dr. Fuller perceived the needs of the multitudes staring death in the face. Along with his messages about eternity, he instructed his music director to include in every broadcast no fewer than three songs about heaven.

Death is just as stark now as it was then. As I write this book, our nation is in a protracted struggle against terrorism. Thousands have already died. Could it be that what grieving or frightened people need to hear is not one more positive pep talk but a message of assurance that, for the follower of Jesus, there is a far better life after this one?

This Year's Model or Historic Faith?

Author and speaker Morton Kelsey used a dramatic visual to drive home the importance of eternity. He took scissors and a New Testament and cut out every verse dealing with the invisible world. The pages barely held together. He had excised one-third of its seven thousand verses. Kelsey displayed his shredded Bible as a stark reminder of how far we have strayed from the emphasis of the New Testament.

Why does heaven seem to have no allure for most of us? Philip Yancey suggests several reasons.[4] One, he explains, is that many Americans are affluent enough to buy whatever they want; earlier generations looked to heaven for this abundance of luxuries. During the Great Depression of the 1930s, for instance, many escaped to the movies to live vicariously in southern mansions or New York penthouses. Others faced this life squarely in hopes of a better life to come.

The decades have taken the edge off acute hunger and poverty for many (but not all) Americans. Reinforced by a relentless marketing blitz that assures us that we can have heaven on Earth (provided we use the coolest products), many simply don't want to opt for a heaven they haven't seen when they *have* seen Beverly Hills.

A further result of our ravenous consumerism is that "the older images of heaven, the biblical ones, have lost their appeal." Streets paved with gold may not be the most practical surface for Porsches. It's sadly ironic. This generation has little interest in mansions of unspeakable splendor that will never devalue or deteriorate. Yet they are overly impressed with the cool "cribs" of the rich, famous, and ungodly.

Yancey also suggests that many are indifferent to the afterlife because "a creeping paganism" convinces us that death is the final end of life. Plus, the more our faith is enmeshed with materialism, the more it is akin to paganism. These days we seem to hear fifty messages on "How to Get What You Want From God" for every one message on "How God Can Get What He Wants From You." Incredibly, the more rapidly we race toward the end times and judgment, the less we are exhorted to "prepare to meet your God."[5]

Even some who claim to believe the Bible appear to question the reality of coming judgment. Yet neither Scripture nor the church's historic posture on this subject leaves any doubt as to the final destiny of those without Christ. Scripture clearly describes a coming apocalypse "when the Lord Jesus is revealed from heaven with His mighty angels, in flaming fire taking vengeance on those who do not know God, and on those who do not obey the gospel of our Lord Jesus Christ. These shall be punished with everlasting destruction from the presence of the Lord and from the glory of His power" (2 Thess. 1:7–9).

Polycarp, one of the early church fathers, faced a vicious martyrdom in a Roman arena with wild beasts. The proconsul urged this elderly Christian to renounce his faith in Christ, but to no avail. Finally the Roman official threatened, "If you despise the wild beasts, I will cause you to be consumed with fire, unless you repent [change your mind]." Polycarp replied, "You threaten that fire which burns for a season and after a little while is quenched: for you are ignorant of the fire of the future judgment and eternal punishment, which is reserved for the ungodly."[6] Polycarp, having already given himself up for dead, sought only the salvation of his executioner.

To the testimony of Scripture and countless Christian martyrs, the historic creeds of the church add their affirmation of a real heaven and a real hell. One of the great theological documents of history is the Westminster Confession. This statement of faith clearly declares, "But the wicked who know not God, and obey not the Gospel of Jesus Christ, shall be cast into eternal torments, and be punished with everlasting destruction from the presence of the Lord, and from the glory of His power."[7]

The Baptist Faith and Message states, "The unrighteous will be consigned to hell, the place of everlasting punishment. The righteous in their resurrected and glorified bodies will receive their reward and will dwell forever in heaven with the Lord."[8] The Statement of Fundamental Truths of the Assemblies of God declares, "Whosoever is not found written in the Book of Life, together with the devil and his angels, the beast and the false prophet, will be consigned to everlasting punishment in the lake which burneth with fire and brimstone, which is the second death."[9]

It is not that we have formally removed our belief in heaven and hell. It is simply that there is an eerie silence, even among evangelicals, as many sort out in their heart of hearts what they really hold to be true. But in the midst of changing attitudes and times, Scripture has not changed. No matter what may be politically or theologically correct in our culture, we have not been authorized to amend Scripture. We are only authorized to proclaim it.

THE SECRET OF LIVING FOREVER

Comedian George Burns quipped, "The secret of living forever is to live to be one hundred—because very few people die after they're one hundred!" (He almost made it.)

We don't like to think that death is an appointed experience for each of us. We want to avoid death. We want to live forever. Actually, the secret of living forever is not to avoid death but to prepare for it. And the proper preparation is by no means morbid. In fact, to be properly prepared to die launches you into a life of freedom and joy.

If you would know the secret of living forever, you must ask what constitutes eternal life. And Jesus (the ultimate authority on living forever) gives the answer. "And this is eternal life," He prayed to His Father, "that they may know You, the only true God, and Jesus Christ whom You have sent" (John 17:3). To know Jesus Christ is to be steeped in life—abundant and eternal life.

One night evangelist Billy Sunday found himself in a seedy section of Chicago. Turning compassionately to a group involved in degrading activities, he said, "Men, why don't you live the way you know you want to die?" We are prepared to live only if we are prepared to die. Thus prepared, not only does the Christian anticipate meeting God in heaven, but also his earthly life teems with experiences where he is meeting God at every turn.

One early Christian bishop offered this succinct eulogy of Christians thrown to lions for sport: "Our people die well." To live well is to know God through the gateway of His Son—not just in a superficial way, but in an ever-deepening commitment of love. This kind of love relationship was common among early believers. They longed to go to heaven because they longed to be with Jesus. They knew that when they were reunited with Him, they would forever be "at home."

> We know that as long as we live in these bodies we are not at home with the Lord. That is why we live by believing and not by seeing. Yes, we are fully confident, and we would rather be away from these bodies, for then we will be at home with the Lord.
> —2 CORINTHIANS 5:6–8, NLT

Where would you rather be *right now*? First-century believers would have had no hesitation. "For me," Paul wrote, "living is for Christ, and dying is even better" (Phil. 1:21, NLT).

AN ABUNDANT ENTRANCE

Second Peter 1:11 in the King James Version translates "a rich welcome" as "an abundant entrance." There's an abundant entrance into heaven for those who live well. Bottom line, living well is living for Jesus. When He returns—and He *will* return—how will you greet Him? He may come for you at the hour of your death, or you may be alive to witness His return to the earth. Either way, He's coming for you. Are you ready to meet Him?

Let's be clear. You qualify to go to heaven by turning away from your sins and placing your faith in Christ as your Savior and Lord. A place in heaven isn't earned; it has already been purchased for you by Jesus through His blood. But you must receive the gift. So, being rightly related to God through faith in His Son qualifies you for heaven. But that does not, in and of itself, ensure that you will fare well when you stand before the Lord to give an account of your life. That requires a day-by-day surrender to His lordship in all areas of your life.

Contemporary Christian music pioneer John Fischer remembers that in the early days of the Jesus Movement all the buzz was about Jesus coming back. The constant challenge was to be ready for His return. Fischer asks, "What keeps us from being ready? We are no longer ready when we have made too many alliances with this world. When all our hopes and dreams and goals and desires are found here on earth, we are no longer interested in looking for the Lord's return.... The safest thing to do in any generation is to simply get ready."[10]

When Jesus returns, not all Christians will greet Him with the same enthusiasm. John warns, "And now, little children, abide in Him, that when He appears, we may have confidence and not be ashamed before Him at His coming" (1 John 2:28). When the Lord Jesus comes back, how will you welcome Him?

The most wonderful blessing in my life other than Jesus is Naomi, my wife of thirty-five years. Because of the nature of the ministry in my stewardship, I am sometimes away from her for two weeks or even longer, often on the other side of the world. Through the years our commitment to one another has produced a deep level of trust. When I read Proverbs 31, I'm reading a description of my wife and our relationship: "The heart of her husband safely trusts her" (v. 11).

Many couples who have to sometimes travel apart from each other are not so fortunate. Suspicion reigns. If, for example, a husband were to return after a long trip and find his wife strangely evasive and "ashamed before him," he would suspect unfaithfulness. With the church, the bride of Christ, it's the same. Those who will blush at His return—those who will be "ashamed before Him"—are the spiritually unfaithful. They have had affairs of the heart, loving the world and the things that are in the world.[11] Some professing Christians will not welcome the Lord with open faces, but rather they will hide their faces from Him.

To continue the illustration, suppose a returning husband got this kind of reception from his wife: "Boy, am I glad to see you! Look at this place. Everything's a mess. I just haven't found time to do any of those things you wanted me to do. I'm so glad you're back. I need a permanent vacation. You take it from here; *you* fix it."

How do you think the husband would take such a "welcome"? Yet many Christians anticipate Christ's return primarily as an escape from this world's pressures. They see no need to work for a better world; they're content to just let Jesus "fix it" when He comes back. Their frazzled lives are often a jumbled mess of "urgent" involvements while they consistently give concerns of timeless importance low priority.

Suppose a returning husband were to discover his wife had been completely unproductive while he was away. "I just waited for you to come back and take care of things. You're so much better at handling things than I am. So I just kicked back and TiVo-ed 'til the trumpet." If you really want to get Jesus angry, that would be the way to do it. He even told a story about such poor stewardship and how the returning man in charge would deal with his unfruitful stewards. It's not a pretty picture. Jesus compared some of His people who just chose to clock out early with a man who buried his talent in the ground. To put it mildly, the landlord dealt severely with this person and called him "wicked and lazy" (Matt. 25:26).

But what if the husband returns to find the house and all the family concerns in order? In fact, his wife has wisely invested the assets and multiplied them. She has responded to those important things the husband asked to be accomplished while he was away. When he returns she greets him with a joyous, "Welcome back. I love you."

The husband would be thrilled to return to such a bride.

COME, LORD JESUS

Now, what kind of bride do you think Jesus wants to come back to? No doubt the one who has done what He asked her to do. And He left us a Great Commission to get the gospel to every person on the earth and turn the nations into His disciples. We dare not occupy our lives with so many other things (even good things) that we fail to give ourselves to the one clear thing He left us to get done.

You are of infinite worth to God and to His plan for your generation. So don't slowly drown your life in trivia. Oswald Chambers said, "One individual life may be of priceless value to God's purposes, and yours may be that life."[12] God's purposes in any generation are fulfilled by people—people who are poised to hear and obey His agenda for their times. We cannot allow ourselves to be drugged into indifference by multiple hours of entertainment or other distractions. Too many Christians are googling their way to glory without a clue as to what God is up to or how He wants to use them. The challenge for us today is to rip away from the trivia trap and sensitize ourselves to heaven's directives.

But this means heaven must become real to us and the return of Christ must return to center stage in our hearts and hopes. Hudson Taylor, pioneer missionary to China and founder of China Inland Mission, wrote, "I saw…that all through the New Testament the coming of the Lord was the strongest motive for consecration and service, and the greatest comfort in trial and affliction. I learned too that the period of His return for His people was not revealed, the important thing being to be so ready for Him as to be able, whenever He might appear, to give an account of one's stewardship with joy, and not with grief."[13]

Just think how much God loves you and trusts you to commit the bearing of His name to you in these inaugural years of this new millennium. Not only that, but also think of what you have seen and will yet see that godly men and women of the past longed to see but never experienced. "Many prophets and righteous men longed to see what you see but did not see it, and to hear what you hear but did not hear it" (Matt. 13:17, NIV). Without a doubt, "you are a chosen generation, a royal priesthood, a holy nation, His own special people, that you may proclaim the praises of Him who called you out of darkness into His marvelous light" (1 Pet. 2:9).

In classic English understatement, Samuel Johnson, commenting on a man who was expecting to be hanged the next day, wrote, "The prospect of death wonderfully concentrates the mind."[14] Do you need to clear the fog and focus on the big issues? Well, "the prospect of death wonderfully concentrates the mind." Just get ready. Many people today either pretend death will never happen or they have a macabre obsession with it. The Bible calls you to a clearer course than either of these extremes. Just prepare to meet your God. And by doing so, prepare for a life of uncluttered joy—for the priorities in such a life are clear and few. It boils down to pleasing Jesus, just living in light of His coming.

In seminary I took a course in evangelism under an extraordinary man during the last semester he was able to teach. Dr. Oscar Thompson was dying of cancer—no, he was living with cancer. I remember how he lived and taught with such joy, brilliance—and pain. Limping into class and then leaning heavily on his cane, he was a beautiful anomaly. He wanted to press as much of life as possible into his short remaining time, yet he retained a holy nonchalance about temporal things. He made a lasting impression and taught us an axiom I'll always remember: "God doesn't give you dying grace on nondying days." Until his last breath Dr. Thompson had a fragrant grace for living. Then on promotion day he received dying grace—and a rich welcome.

CHAPTER THREE

You Can Only Imagine

Let not your heart be troubled; you believe in God, believe also in Me. In My Father's house are many mansions; if it were not so, I would have told you. I go to prepare a place for you. And if I go and prepare a place for you, I will come again and receive you to Myself, that where I am, there you may be also.

—John 14:1–3

It becomes us to spend this life only as a journey toward heaven... to which we should subordinate all other concerns of life. Why should we labor for or set our hearts on anything else, but that which is our proper end, and true happiness?[1]

—Jonathan Edwards

In the movie *Gladiator*, General Decimus Meridius is seen giving his cavalry a final encouragement to fight well in their battle that will soon begin against Germania. Addressing his troops, he calls on them to give their all in the battle. He challenges them with this profound reminder: "What we do in life echoes in eternity."

It's difficult for us to picture heaven since all our experience is earthbound and time-bound. And because all our experiences involve us directly, it becomes quite a challenge to imagine a place where God is central, not man. But there is indeed such a place. In fact, a slice of heaven is transplanted in us when we crown Jesus as King over our lives. For then, although imperfectly, we come under the same rulership as heaven. Our existence is no longer measured by time; we have embarked on eternal life.

Ken Gire observes, "All we see before us are merely pencil sketches of the world beyond us. Every person is a stick-figured image of God; every place of natural beauty, a charcoal rendering of Paradise; every pleasure, a flat and faded version of the Joy that awaits us."[2]

Let's see if we can get a clearer picture of heaven.

GLIMPSES OF ETERNITY

Many people claim to have had a glimpse of heaven and are beginning to feel freer to describe their out-of-body experiences. For a culture baptized in rationalism, both Christians and non-Christians often tend to take such stories with at least a pretty good-sized grain of salt. But the evidence seems to be mounting that Jesus is giving some people sneak previews of their heavenly home.

For instance, Choo Thomas, a Korean American, shares several direct encounters she says she has had with Jesus. In some of these visitations Choo relates that she was transported directly to heaven where she experienced scenes of indescribable splendor. Some may question these experiences, but Choo has never been the same. "From that day forward I have felt like I'm living more in heaven than on earth," Choo writes. "My visits to heaven have wrought permanent changes in my life. I don't even require as much sleep as I used to, because I feel supernaturally energized by power from on high. Truly, I know that *heaven is so real*, and this makes all the difference in the world."[3]

Then there's the amazing story of Baptist pastor Don Piper. As he was driving home from a conference, his car was crushed by a semi that crossed into his lane. Medical personnel said he died instantly. Yet while his body lay lifeless inside the ruins of his car, Piper says he experienced some of the glories of heaven.

Heaven was many things, but without a doubt, it was the greatest family reunion of all. Everything I experienced was like a first-class buffet for the senses. I had never felt such powerful embraces or feasted my eyes on such beauty. Heaven's light and texture defy earthly eyes or explanation. Warm, radiant light engulfed me. As I looked around, I could hardly grasp the vivid, dazzling colors. Every hue and tone surpassed anything I had ever seen.

With all the heightened awareness of my senses, I felt as if I had never seen, heard or felt anything so real before....Never, even in my happiest moments, had I ever felt so fully alive.[4]

Today Piper admits to some frustration as he tries to relate his brief ninety-minute interlude with eternity. "As I try to explain this, my words seem weak and hardly adequate, because I have to use earthly terms to refer to unimaginable joy, excitement, warmth, and total happiness."[5]

Did you notice the two little words both Choo and Don used to describe heaven? *So real.* It is this life that is less real because it is transitory. It is heaven that is *so real.*

These experiences coincide with John's revelation of this eternal, magnificent city.

The city had no need of the sun or of the moon to shine in it, for the glory of God illuminated it. The Lamb is its light....There shall be no night there: They need no lamp nor light of the sun, for the Lord God gives them light.

—Revelation 21:23; 22:5

In describing part of God's character, the Bible says, "God is light and in Him is no darkness at all" (1 John 1:5). Since this heavenly city is God's abode, it follows that there is no night; there is only constant light and, therefore, constant revelation and illumination. What a conducive climate for growth!

BLUEPRINT OF HEAVEN

For many years R. G. Lee was the senior pastor of the famous Bellevue Baptist Church in Memphis. Dr. Lee was one of the last of the great Southern orator-preachers. His command of the English language was, perhaps, unexcelled by any preacher in American history. When he was well into his eighties I had the privilege of hearing him preach on heaven. I've never heard a more beautiful sermon. He said with grace and eloquence what I've struggled to say through several drafts of this book. But when Dr. Lee lay on his deathbed, even this master pulpiteer was at a loss for words. He would weave in and out of consciousness with looks of rapture on his aged face. Intermittently he would say, "Oh, look! Look!" Returning briefly to consciousness, he told his attending nurse, "I wanted so badly to help people see heaven when I preached. But, oh, I never did it justice."

So we must see even biblical definitions of heaven, though true, as mere accommodations to our limited ability to grasp its beauty. But let's stretch our hearts and minds and let God's Word describe something of the scope of this eternal city.[6] According to Scripture, this heavenly city is an enormously massive cube, 12,000 furlongs in length, breadth, and height. A furlong is 582-1/2 feet, or approximately 1/8 of a mile. So the dimensions of this city are roughly 1,500 miles in all directions. If this city were set on United States territory, it would extend from the northern tip of Maine to the southernmost point of Florida and would reach from the Atlantic Ocean to the Colorado River. If it were placed over Europe, it would cover all of England, France, Germany, Italy, the Eastern European countries, and about half of Russia. The surface level of this New Jerusalem is a staggering 2,250,000 square miles. Talk about property value!

But that is only the measurement of the first level! The Bible says that the city is as high as it is wide. It is not a square but a cube. Think of a building fifteen hundred miles high! But this is not a building; it's an entire city built layer upon layer to this incredible height.

The Bible says there are streets in this city, so let's assume that they are laid out on a square grid at one-mile intervals. (This would be far less frequent than any city on the earth.) Such a grid would give us 3,000 streets per level, each one 1,500 miles long for a total street length of 4,500,000 miles per level. If we assume each level will be one mile above the preceding one, there could be as many as 1,500 of these levels, thereby giving the city over 6,750,000,000 (that's six billion seven hundred fifty million) miles of roads—all paved with pure gold!

Now to the jasper walls surrounding the first level. They are a half-mile high! This is far higher than any church spire in the world. The gates themselves are solid pearls. The city contains three and one-third billion cubic miles! Even if half of this area were allowed for streets, it would still leave room for nine quadrillion rooms thirty feet long, thirty feet wide, and thirty feet high. Believe me—there's room for you!

Why not stop for a few minutes and engage in some "sanctified daydreaming"?

> Surrounded by Your glory, what will my heart feel?
> Will I dance for You, Jesus, or in awe of You be still?
> Will I stand in Your presence, or to my knees will I fall?
> Will I sing, "Hallelujah"? Will I be able to speak at all?
> I can only imagine! I can only imagine![7]

SOMETHING TO OCCUPY YOUR TIME

No doubt the God of design and economy has clear uses for the vast expanses of this heavenly city. Surely the same Lord who had His disciples gather up the twelve baskets of food fragments "so that nothing will be wasted" does not wish for these massive amounts of space to go unoccupied. So with what are these "cubicles" to be filled? Redeemed people and fantastic ideas! And Scripture teaches that there will be a new earth in which these ideas can be implemented. Most people have gone to their graves still grappling for solutions to puzzling predicaments. But for those who die in Christ, the process of thinking continues with none of the limitations or impossibilities we struggled with on Earth!

For many years the Brill Building in New York City housed many of the most creative writing teams in popular music. Memorable melodies and lyrics were incubated in sparse little rooms with just an upright piano, a table, and a couple of chairs. Still, the creativity flowed, because very creative people were huddled together. Now, imagine a place of architectural perfection where all the stops are pulled out on your creativity and you have infinite energy, clarity, and resources. You're occupying vast rooms with many other redeemed and totally unrestricted Jesus worshipers. God-honoring ideas explode! This new earth will be fully under Christ's sovereignty, so world hunger is solved in seconds. Diseases are forever a thing of the past. Poverty and its roots are obliterated. That's just for starters. You embark on the most gratifying work ever, cooperating with God in constructing "a new heaven and a new earth." "Father & Sons" are now eternally in business together. We can only imagine!

Far from being a place to recline on a cloud playing endless stanzas of "elevator music" on a harp, heaven is a place of inexpressible creativity and joy. We are most joyful and fulfilled when we are productive. As C. S. Lewis said, "Joy is the serious business of Heaven."[8] In fact, "no eye has seen, no ear has heard, and no mind has imagined what God has prepared for those who love him" (1 Cor. 2:9, NLT).

We will continue to develop, learn, and serve, since servanthood, motivated by love, is the normal standard of conduct in this new scheme of things. In Aldous Huxley's *Brave New World*, torture and inhumane actions are the norm.[9] But in this truly brave new world, love motivates unselfish service.

Imagine a place of architectural perfection where all the stops are pulled out on creativity. Joseph Bayle, now living in heaven, described a fictitious (or is it?) scene in which he would ask the Lord for assistance in being acclimated to this new love-environment.

"This work You mentioned earlier. Will it just be managing Your universe?"

"Of course not. You can also plant a garden—without sweat or drought or weeds. Like Eden. You can create a poem or an oratorio. You can carve wood or paint a landscape."

"To praise You."

"Everything in heaven is to My praise. My people intend it so. I accept it but that doesn't mean they only sing My praise—their work is praise to Me."

"Will I be able to sing? I always wanted to."

"Handel's choir always has room for one more. But for that matter, you may want to have your own choir, to learn to conduct it—or an orchestra."[10]

Then there is the concept of a timeless eternity—an infinity of "time" (or more precisely the lack of it) in which to experiment with God's ongoing creation and to explore the depths of His character. Bound as we are to time, it is difficult even to begin to perceive an existence out of the realms of time. Scientists, however, are beginning to probe this possibility—just a little. While the idea of literal time travel is still viewed by most as improbable, Einstein has taught us that time is not fixed; it is relative. At the speed of light the passage of time vanishes. Thus we speak now of "time warps" and "freeze frames." Could it be that in that new world we will travel at—or even beyond—the speed of light?

Years ago Paul Billheimer taught that engaging in victorious prayer now is training for eternity. He called prayer "on the job training for ruling and reigning with Christ."[11] And when we develop our talents as well, we're preparing for something even greater. Church consultant Reggie McNeal notes, "I believe we will carry our talent into eternity. (Since the Bible clearly teaches that our personalities and ethnicities remain intact in heaven, why not the talent we have been given?) I suspect there are uses for our talent that we have not yet imagined. We are practicing for eternity when we practice our talent."[12]

"But," some will protest, "you can be so heavenly minded you're no earthly good." This refers to the notion that Christians might expend such energy concentrating on heaven that they fail in their responsibilities here on Earth. Frankly, I've never met anyone like that. In fact, I think just the opposite happens. Heavenly minded people seldom retreat to ivory towers. Rather, it is usually the heavenly minded who are most ready to roll up their sleeves and get to work on the problems of Earth.

Look, for instance, at Mother Teresa and Mark Buntain—two "heavenly minded" sojourners who gave their lives for the diseased and impoverished of Kolkata (formerly Calcutta). Remember the "heavenly minded" Wilberforce whose passion for human dignity forced eradication of slavery throughout the British Empire. Go to the sleazy underworld of Hollywood and watch the tireless workers at the Dream Center as they tell inquiring street people how to get to heaven while providing them food and shelter on the way. Scan the world, and see Christian compassion that has spawned thousands of hospitals, shelters, clinics, children's homes, schools, and colleges—all built in heaven's honor. The point is obvious. Those who truly set their sights on another world are usually the most active for constructive change in this one.

C. S. Lewis said, "The Apostles themselves, who set on foot the conversion of the Roman Empire, the great men who built up the Middle Ages, the English Evangelicals who abolished the Slave Trade, all left their mark on Earth, precisely because their minds were occupied with Heaven. It is since Christians have largely ceased to think of the other world that they have become so ineffective in this one."[13]

HEAVEN ON EARTH

The Bible says, "Here we have no continuing city, but we seek the one to come" (Heb. 13:14). Indeed, nothing here is permanent. Think back on your high school graduation. Do you remember signing the yearbooks and promising always to stay in touch? Did they? Did you? In a ten-year span most of the key players in your life (except your family) could well change. And tragically for many, the key players of family itself will also change. We have no continuing city.

The transient nature of life is a powerful incentive to live for eternity. But this does not nullify our responsibilities on this planet. The Christian holds his desire for another world with his stewardship in this world in tandem. Calvin Miller was right when he said, "We are living in honor of the next world while keeping our arms embraced around this one."[14]

God's Word is clear that we are currently engaged in a cooperative effort with Him in the establishment of His purposes on the earth. While I claim no rare insights into eschatology, I do not believe Jesus was speaking tongue-in-cheek when He taught us to pray, "Your kingdom come. Your will be done *on earth* as it is in heaven" (Matt. 6:10, emphasis added). Surely He meant for us to pray in faith for results we could see not only in a coming kingdom but also in our lifetimes.

Heaven has already established countless beachheads on Earth. Each time someone receives Jesus as Lord of his or her life, a beachhead for the kingdom of God is established. At its essence, the kingdom of God is simply the unrivaled rule of God. Not only is His kingdom coming, but it has already come in hearts all over the world.

Augustine spoke of this dual citizenship of Christians in his classic treatise *City of God*. He affirmed that Christians do have a responsibility to earthly authorities but that their higher loyalty is to Jesus Christ. Whenever the two cities—the temporal City of Man and the eternal City of God—collide in a conflict of values or power, the Christian is always to align with the eternal.[15]

Many Bible scholars conclude that there will be a constant interplay between heaven and Earth. In fact, some feel that the majority of our "time" will be spent cultivating a perfectly restored Planet Earth. Martyn Lloyd-Jones wrote, "Everything will be glorified, even nature itself. And that seems to me to be the biblical teaching about the eternal state: that what we call heaven is life in this perfect world as God intended humanity to live it....Men and women are meant to live in the body, and will live in a glorified body in a glorified world, and God will be with them."[16]

Jack Hayford concurs. "At the end of time a new heaven will be created to surround the new earth," he writes. "This new heaven will be the place of God's perfect presence (Isa. 65:17; 66:22; Rev. 21:1). Then there will be a literal fulfillment of heaven on earth."[17]

Theologian Wayne Grudem writes, "There will be new heavens and a new earth—an entirely renewed creation—and we will live with God there....There will also be a new kind of unification of heaven and earth....There will be a joining of heaven and earth in this new creation."[18]

THE CELESTIAL CITY

Heaven is more solid than Earth's matter, more sure for the Christian than tomorrow's sunrise. It is a place where wounds are healed forever, hearts mended permanently, and hopes realized eternally.

> And God will wipe away every tear from their eyes; there shall be no more death, nor sorrow, nor crying; and there shall be no more pain, for the former things have passed away.
>
> —REVELATION 21:4

Passed away! On this earth when we say someone has "passed away," we are endeavoring to soften the thud of death's reality. But in heaven it is death itself that has passed away and, with death's demise, all of Earth's attending sorrows. Within every Christian believer there is a slight holy discomfort that can sometimes become very pronounced. It's a yearning for our eternal home with God. Abraham felt this longing. "He was looking forward to the city with foundations, whose architect and builder is God" (Heb. 11:10, NIV).

Commenting on the fact of heaven, Edith Schaeffer observed, "This is reality. Heaven is a place. There is a city we are going to see and walk in. Neither the place, nor the singing instead of the sighing, nor the pleasure instead of the pain, is an illusion. We await that which is *real.*"[19]

I wonder if there is not a skeptic who is doubting as she reads, or a seeker who is hoping against hope that it may be true. Let me assure you that it is true. If it were false, there could be no true Christianity. Indeed, this is a great part of the reason for Christianity's collapse in liberal circles, for a Christianity without eternity is a Christianity with the life ripped out. Then our faith would no longer truly be faith; it would merely be one of dozens of competing moralistic philosophies.

C. S. Lewis stated bluntly, "We are very shy nowadays of even mentioning Heaven. We are afraid of the jeer about 'pie in the sky,' and of being told that we are trying to 'escape' from the duty of making a happy world here and now into the dreams of a happy world elsewhere. But either there is 'pie in the sky' or there is not. If there is not, then Christianity is false, for this doctrine is woven into its whole fabric. If there is, then this truth, like any other, must be faced."[20]

Have you faced this truth? Are you living in the joy and anticipation of this truth? Preparation for heaven begins now. And, yes, the key component is faith—faith in the sacrifice of Jesus on the cross for your sins. When you actually believe that He took *your* place, dying the death you deserved, and when you open your life to His loving control, heaven will open its gates to you. You have a sure hope.

> Let us then be true and faithful,
> Trusting, serving every day;
> Just one glimpse of Him in glory
> Will the toils of life repay.
> When we all get to heaven,
> What a day of rejoicing that will be!
> When we all see Jesus,
> We'll sing and shout the victory.[21]

CHAPTER FOUR

HEAVEN: THE SAFEST INVESTMENT ON EARTH

For our citizenship is in heaven, from which we also eagerly wait for the Savior, the Lord Jesus Christ, who will transform our lowly body that it may be conformed to His glorious body, according to the working by which He is able even to subdue all things to Himself.

—PHILIPPIANS 3:20–21

There have been times when I think we do not desire heaven but more often I find myself wondering whether, in our heart of hearts, we have ever desired anything else.[1]

—C. S. LEWIS

IN 1801 ON A SUNDAY MORNING IN CANE RIDGE, KENTUCKY, AN unknown preacher stood on a fallen tree before thousands at an open-air camp meeting. He took as his text 2 Corinthians 5:10 (KJV), "We must all appear before the judgment seat of Christ." Suddenly an awesome conviction of sin settled on the crowd as the impact of their future accountability to God blanketed them. Hundreds instinctively fell to the ground, crying to God for mercy and forgiveness.

Sometimes called the Cane Ridge Revival, this awesome gathering triggered America's Second Great Awakening. These early Americans had gathered to hear from God. When He spoke to them through His Word, He pointed them toward ultimate things. But many today are so engrossed in today's imperatives that they would never think of carving out time to pursue God and lay up treasures in heaven. Yet their personal, final exam before Jesus is, at the most, just a few years off.

Someone has suggested that architecture throughout history says a lot about our values. For hundreds of years the tallest structures were churches with their high steeples, acting as a pointed reminder to set our affections heavenward. But for the last hundred years mighty skyscrapers have eclipsed even the most impressive church buildings. They are modern man's new temples. The inferred message of these imposing structures is that money and materialism now reign. You need look no higher than the building itself. You can have heaven on earth.

Yet those very buildings house businesses that are frighteningly fragile. Greed has caught up with our ever-expanding gross domestic product (GDP), and now a "post-Enron era" has thrown a pall of fear over the marketplace. Trusting investors have watched their hopes and fortunes evaporate. Now suspicion has misplaced trust. Jesus predicted this would happen just prior to His return: "Sin will be rampant everywhere," He warned, "and the love of many will grow cold" (Matt. 24:12, NLT).

It would be misleading to suggest that only the ungodly have lost their economic equilibrium. Many honest, hard-working Christians have suffered terribly. Families' prospects have been hurt. Churches and ministries have reeled from the double-barrel blast of Christians' diminished financial capabilities and widely publicized scandals. From a natural viewpoint, dread would be in order.

The Bible cautions against the tendency to wrap our hearts around money and things it can buy: "Do not love the world or the things in the world. If anyone loves the world, the love of the Father is not in him" (1 John 2:15, NIV). Jesus taught by word and humble example, "One's life does not consist in the abundance of the things he possesses" (Luke 12:15). Jesus told the story of a man who was so affluent he didn't know where to put all his money. He finally determined to tear down his barns and build bigger ones (no doubt with higher fences to better isolate him from the plight of the poor). Jesus blatantly denounced this man as a shortsighted fool and warns, "So is he who lays up treasures for himself, and is not rich toward God" (Luke 12:21).

ECONOMIC UNCERTAINTY AND TRUE RICHES

If these reminders seem brusque, perhaps it is because I am writing this chapter from a small wooden desk in rural India. When the electricity works I use my host's computer (on which was slapped a large tax since it is a "luxury item"). When the electric current is cut without notice (a frequent occurrence), I write longhand. As I look outside I see grass huts, low-caste workers who farm the fields for a few hundred dollars per year, and an ox-driven cart carrying the day's harvest to market.

"But," you may protest, "that's not the real world." Then why is ours the "real world"? Only a fraction of this planet's population knows our world with its mutual funds and retirement plans. Three billion people live in theirs with its constricting and unflinching needs.

My heart aches for the people I see outside my window. I look at their grass and bamboo dwellings and wonder what happens when the rainy season comes. I ponder what it's like to drink only typhoid-infested water. How does food taste that is prepared on an open fire fueled by dried cow dung? What is it like to have children with intellectual promise who cannot possibly hope for a decent education? How deeply dehumanizing is it to wake day after day, year after year, to these same debilitating conditions as your parents did before you and as your children will after you? And in the midst of such intense, immediate despair, what is it like to have no hope of heaven, no good news of salvation, no forgiveness, no Jesus?

When things are viewed from both a global and an eternal perspective, many of our preconceived notions must bow to reality. Most of the world now, including the United States, is in economic disarray. Our national debt has spiraled completely out of control. Yet no one seems to know how to stop feeding this materialistic monster we've created. And this "monster" is us. Jesus predicted such a time when there would be "distress of nations, with perplexity" (Luke 21:25). The inference from the original language is that there is no way out. It is no longer the religious fanatics and self-styled prophets who lead the parade forecasting doom. Experts in economics and sociology postulate that we may have reached the point of no return. We are literally drowning in red ink.

Our national sins (as well as our personal ones) certainly justify the judgment of God. As Christians, however, we do not give in to despair. God has a propensity for mercy when His children cry out to Him in repentance. Throughout history, God has relented from even His pronounced judgment in response to the sincere cries of the penitent. I am frankly encouraged as I see intensive, focused prayer springing up across America. This signals coming revival, in spite of the storm clouds.

It is true that many godly people are prophesying doom. Even if they are hearing correctly, it is not unprecedented for God to take a merciful course in response to brokenness and prayer. God has promised, "The instant I speak concerning a nation and concerning a kingdom, to pluck up, to pull down, and to destroy it, if that nation against whom I have spoken turns from its evil, I will relent of the disaster that I thought to bring upon it" (Jer. 18:7–8).

Through all our heartbreaking sins and scandals God is speaking clearly. He is calling His church to repentance and holiness. He is wooing us away from the lust of the flesh, the lust of the eyes, and the pride of life. That is why a new look at an eternal perspective is so timely. God is calling us to a new definition of success.

William James, a noted psychologist at the turn of the century, possessed keen insight into the coming crisis of moral weakness that would confront America. In a letter to H. G. Wells, dated September 11, 1906, he spoke almost prophetically of our battle of will. He pointedly blasted "the moral flabbiness born of the exclusive worship of…SUCCESS. That—with the squalid cash interpretation put on the word success—is our national disease."[2]

No preacher could have been more on target. Now God Himself is calling His church to raise a standard of righteousness. A groundswell of cries for holiness and justice is beginning to be heard throughout the land. To preserve any semblance of civilization as we have known it, there must be a moral revolution.

Jesus is always in the business of reconciliation and restoration. Just as the powerful Wesleyan movement swept Britain in a tide of salvation and sanctification, our times cry out for another even larger dose of biblical holiness. I'm convinced it can come—and quickly. What has taken the devil years to unravel slowly, Jesus Christ can restore in minutes. The road to full restoration may be long, but repentance itself happens in a moment. Then God's mercy responds immediately and restoration begins.

A schoolboy was telling his classmates about the wonderful difference in his family since his father had become a Christian. Before his conversion, his father had terrorized the family with his alcoholism, breaking lamps and throwing chairs in his tirades. But now Christ had delivered him, and peace prevailed in the home. He even used the money once spent on alcohol to help redecorate their home.

The boy's teacher, a skeptical postmodern, overheard his happy testimony. Wishing to "enlighten" him, she said, "Johnny, you can't hope for a lasting change. Your father has just had a traumatic religious experience. Besides, you can't believe in a religion based on the Bible with all its myths. You don't believe that story about Jesus turning the water into wine, do you?"

"Why shouldn't I?" Johnny replied. "When Jesus came to my house He turned beer into furniture!"

Jesus Christ is the radical reformer—of persons, of families, of nations, of destinies. He wants to invade your life and your thinking, even as you read. He stands ready to adjust our perspective—to His.

INVESTING IN ETERNITY

Living *now* for rewards *then* is especially challenging for this generation that is steeped in instant gratification. But if we view this life as a sort of boot camp for the afterlife, our perceptions—and our actions—will change. Our true allegiance will be to the kingdom of heaven. Phillip Yancey writes:

> The kingdom of heaven recasts life on this planet from Jesus' own perspective, the perspective of two worlds. His words seem revolutionary to us only because we think like people who live an average of sixty or seventy years on a planet made of rocks and trees and soil. Jesus introduced a new way of thinking, raising sights to a life that extends into eternity and involves unseen worlds we have not the capacity to detect. He came to establish an alternate community centered on values from that invisible world, "on earth as it is in heaven." Seen in that light, the kingdom of heaven prescribes a way of life that promotes what matters most and lasts longest.[3]

Henry Ward Beecher mused, "Success is full of promise till men get it; and then it is last year's nest from which the bird has flown."[4] This elusive quality of the fulfillment of hopes is a typical phenomenon here on Earth. But not so with heaven's rewards. They are permanent and teeming with undiminished joy. At least eighty times the Bible speaks of rewards. Here is just a sampling of the Bible's urgings for us to seek heaven's nondepreciating accolades.

> Surely there is a reward for the righteous; surely He is God who judges in the earth.
>
> —PSALM 58:11

> The wicked man does deceptive work, but he who sows righteousness will have a sure reward.
>
> —PROVERBS 11:18

Behold, the Lord G<small>OD</small> shall come with a strong hand, and His arm shall rule for Him; behold, His reward is with Him.

—I<small>SAIAH</small> 40:10

Blessed are you when they revile and persecute you, and say all kinds of evil against you falsely for My sake. Rejoice and be exceedingly glad, for great is your reward in heaven.

—M<small>ATTHEW</small> 5:11–12

But when you do a charitable deed, do not let your left hand know what your right hand is doing, that your charitable deed may be in secret; and your Father who sees in secret will Himself reward you openly.

—M<small>ATTHEW</small> 6:3–4

But you, when you pray, go into your room, and when you have shut your door, pray to your Father who is in the secret place; and your Father who sees in secret will reward you openly.

—M<small>ATTHEW</small> 6:6

For the Son of Man will come in the glory of His Father with His angels, and then He will reward each according to his works.

—M<small>ATTHEW</small> 16:27

For whoever gives you a cup of water to drink in My name, because you belong to Christ, assuredly, I say to you, he will by no means lose his reward.

—M<small>ARK</small> 9:41

But love your enemies, do good, and lend, hoping for nothing in return; and your reward will be great.

—L<small>UKE</small> 6:35

And whatever you do, do it heartily, as to the Lord and not to men, knowing that from the Lord you will receive the reward of the inheritance; for you serve the Lord Christ.

—C<small>OLOSSIANS</small> 3:23–24

But recall the former days in which, after you were illuminated, you endured a great struggle with sufferings: partly while you were made a spectacle both by reproaches and tribulations, and partly while you became companions of those who were so treated; for you had compassion on me in my chains, and joyfully accepted the plundering of your goods, knowing that you have a better and an enduring possession for yourselves in heaven. Therefore do not cast away your confidence, which has great reward.

—HEBREWS 10:32–35

Look to yourselves, that we do not lose those things we worked for, but that we may receive a full reward.

—2 JOHN 8

And, behold, I am coming quickly, and My reward is with Me, to give to every one according to his work.

—REVELATION 22:12

Jonathan Edwards, a godly Puritan preacher and also one of the greatest intellects America has produced, determined that he would focus on ultimate success. In his early twenties Edwards compiled a set of personal resolutions. Among them was this commitment: "Resolved, To endeavor to obtain for myself as much happiness, in the other world, as I possibly can."[5] Edwards took seriously Christ's direction to "lay up for yourselves treasures in heaven" (Matt. 6:20).

Those who receive heaven's rich rewards will also be rich in eternal intimacy with God. They will be eternally useful. They are "storing up their treasure as a good foundation for the future so that they may take hold of real life" (1 Tim. 6:19, NLT).

All these injunctions boil down to seeing beyond the present to the eternal, loving God supremely, and serving people as an expression of our love for Him. There is a payoff worth waiting for.

THE PRIZE OF THE HIGH CALLING

Every now and then I run across people who say, "Well, I'm not doing this for rewards. It will be reward enough just to be in heaven."

This misses the whole point—and it's bad theology. Heaven is not a reward; it is part of our redemption gift package when we come to saving faith in Jesus Christ. Further, to place little value on what heaven says has great value insults the very Lord who offers these rewards. Rick Howard and Jamie Lash speak pointedly to this:

> Not concerned about reward? Do you think that just because you get to heaven, everything's going to be fine? Don't you realize the Bible says Jesus will be ashamed of some of us [Mark 8:38]? Don't you realize some of us will shrink back from Him in shame or terror because we're not prepared [1 John 2:28]? You treat God's rewards as if they don't matter, but the Bible says they are worth enduring suffering, false accusation, exclusion and hatred for [Luke 6:22–23]. Indeed, they are worth dying for [Revelation 2:10]![6]

It is never selfish to seek heaven's rewards. In fact, Jesus commands us to seek heaven's treasures in the Sermon on the Mount.[7] It is, as Rick and Jamie write, "a healthy ambition, a holy calling, one that frees us from selfishness. It trains us to seek the pleasure and glory of God."[8]

In the words of Oswald Chambers, we are to give our utmost for His highest. As we yield to each prompting of the Holy Spirit, we are laying up spiritual treasure. The only time we have in which to invest is now, this present moment. You can do nothing about the past except give it to Jesus. Tomorrow is not promised to you. Now is your opportunity, and it is fleeting.

Bruce Wilkinson reminds us, "Every day is a new opportunity to discover what eternal business might be lurking in the ordinary business of being human."[9] In view of the brevity of time we should pray, as David did, "So teach us to number our days, that we may gain a heart of wisdom" (Ps. 90:12). And what will be the result of a heart of wisdom? A prudent walk before the Lord and a conscientious investing of time. "Be very careful, then, how you live—not as unwise but as wise, making the most of every opportunity, because the days are evil" (Eph. 5:15–16, NIV).

And as we invest our days for Him, through worship and service, God's law of sowing and reaping goes into effect. A basic, universal law is that whatever we sow, we reap—sometimes very soon, sometimes years later, sometimes in eternity. But the principle always holds true. We reap what we sow.

A little-known story of two evangelical leaders well illustrates this immutable principle. One night in the mid-1940s, a young college graduate was thumbing a ride to Los Angeles. (It was safe back then to "hitch a ride" from a stranger.) Not a Christian, the young man's goal in life was to become a millionaire and live in Beverly Hills. But this night, the Oklahoma collegian was short on cash.

A man picked up the hitchhiker, and they began to talk. "Do you know anywhere in Los Angeles I can spend the night?" the traveler inquired. "I think so," replied the driver. "There's a guy named Dawson Trotman who's putting up some sailors at his house, teaching them the Bible or something. Maybe he'd find you a bed tonight."

And so it was that on his first night in California Bill Bright received hospitality from Dawson Trotman. When they met, neither man had any way of knowing that within a few years they would both head massively influential Christian ministries.

A decade after that providential night, Trotman's Navigators were in a race against time to purchase Glen Eyrie, their proposed Colorado Springs headquarters. Bill Bright, by now head of the fledgling Campus Crusade for Christ ministry, personally gave sacrificially and wrote five thousand friends of his new organization, asking them to help. The Navigators were able to make the purchase.

Trotman's kindness, sown a decade earlier, was reaped in kindness sown by Bill Bright and Campus Crusade to the sister ministry of the

Navigators. This beautiful picture of deference and secure leadership on both of their parts is a potent example for us today. Little did Dawson and Lila Trotman realize that one night's room and board, given in the name of Jesus, would yield many thousands of dollars years later, when they needed a miracle.[10] In the same way, many cups of cold water given in the natural course of things will be returned in invaluable treasure—both in this life and the next.

Whenever someone with perception says, in effect, "This above all else," it is wise to pay close attention to what the "one thing" is. For instance, in Shakespeare's *Hamlet*, he advises, "This above all: to thine own self be true."[11] More ancient is the counsel attributed to the Seven Sages inscribed at the Delphic Oracle some six hundred years before Christ: "Know thyself."

Sound advice from time-honored wisdom: *Know yourself. Be true to yourself.* But there comes from the pen of a Jewish scholar-turned-apostle an even greater piece of wisdom: Forget the past and *give yourself* to attaining the heavenly prize at the end of life's race. "Brethren, I do not count myself to have apprehended; but one thing I do, forgetting those things which are behind and reaching forward to those things which are ahead, I press toward the goal for the prize of the upward call of God in Christ Jesus" (Phil. 3:13–14). This is to live in heaven's honor.

So press on, with your eyes fixed on the finish line. When the winner stretches forward and finally breaks the tape, it's worth all the effort.

CHAPTER FIVE

By His Wounds

And He cast out the spirits with a word, and healed all who were sick, that it might be fulfilled which was spoken by Isaiah the prophet, saying, "He Himself took our infirmities and bore our sicknesses."

—Matthew 8:16–17

There is a land of pure delight,
Where saints immortal reign,
Infinite day excludes the night,
And pleasures banish pain.[1]

—Isaac Watts

I am the product of a miracle. When I was born, neither my mother nor I was expected to live. At birth I weighed less than four pounds. While my mother was in labor, my father waited anxiously with a family friend, an eminent evangelist who was powerfully used in overseas gospel meetings. His name was T. L. Osborn. There was a complication, and both my mother's life and mine were in jeopardy. Just as I was being born, Dr. Osborn was strongly impressed to pray for my life and my mother's. Turning to my father, he said, "Warren, we've got to rebuke the spirit of death right now."

God intervened. What appeared to be certain death for both of us was turned into victory and honor for the Lord. Today, over five decades later, I enjoy consistently good health. And my mother, now almost ninety, is also in good health.

Remembering that God spared my life at birth has been a strong undercurrent of "knowing" deep in my spirit. I never question that He has a specific will for my life, and death cannot take me until His work for me is accomplished. Jim Elliot put it this way: "I am immortal until my work is finished." Every believer who knows his times are in God's hand has the same assurance.

I share that story to go on record both as a witness and a recipient of the present-day healing power of God. I have experienced the healing virtue of Christ many times. And I've witnessed the dramatic effects of Christ's healing touch in answer to believing prayer. At the core of who I am I know that healing and miracles are to accompany the preaching of the gospel. When Jesus sent His disciples to proclaim the kingdom of God, He also gave them authority over demons and to cure diseases (Luke 9:1–2). When Jesus issued the Great Commission, He promised that wonderful signs would follow those who believe. As those early disciples went out sharing the good news, miracles accompanied their proclamation (Mark 16:15–20). Jesus heals people to verify the fact that He is the living Son of God. But He also heals people just because He loves them.

Having said this, I wish to help those whose healing has been delayed. By suggesting that some healings will be received only in heaven, I will no doubt receive criticism from those who say I lack faith and am insulting the promises of God. If in any way this is my intent, I ask forgiveness, not from my critics, but from God. I want to stimulate faith, not diminish it. I have been privileged to view the issue of healing from a dual perspective. As an evangelist, I have seen remarkable healings and miracles in answer to prayer. But I have also seen those who have left in the same wheelchairs they came in. Toward them I must minister pastorally. Did God fail? Did I fail? Did the person's faith fail? What can you do if healing is delayed?

Is God at Fault?

Let's get one thing straight from the outset: God is good. He does not inflict sickness on anyone. And since God never inflicts sickness on anyone, it cannot be said that sickness itself glorifies God. Now the godly character that is often produced as a result of suffering does glorify God. The very physical weakness we disdain often casts us on God in a greater way. When the body is weak, there is less chance for an unholy brew of flesh and spirit. The inner person of the spirit must compensate for the weakness of the flesh. So while sickness itself is never God honoring, the effects of sickness on the teachable Christian often are.

This is not to say that God allows us to be sick to "teach us a lesson." Remember, His nature is kind and good. God is, however, the master strategist who delights in watching the devil overplay his hand in his tactics against us. What the devil means for evil, God reverses for our good.

When faith is exercised, the result many times is a lifting of oppressing circumstances or a healing from tormenting disease. But God may choose to honor our faith, not by releasing us from our difficulties but by developing Christlikeness in us in the midst of our difficulties. After all, how can we become like Jesus unless we too know something about sorrow and are acquainted with grief?

Some of the most forceful teachings on faith in the Bible come from the pen of the apostle Paul. And his experience backed up his teaching. This mighty apostle, who cast out demons and whose hands were a transmitter for healing from Christ, was no less a person of faith because God chose not to remove his thorn in the flesh. Paul turned this tormenting deficit into one of his greatest assets: "Concerning this thing," Paul wrote, "I pleaded with the Lord three times that it might depart from me. And He said to me, 'My grace is sufficient for you, for My strength is made perfect in weakness.' Therefore most gladly I will rather boast in my infirmities, that the power of Christ may rest upon me. Therefore I take pleasure in infirmities, in reproaches, in needs, in persecutions, in distresses, for Christ's sake. For when I am weak, then I am strong" (2 Cor. 12:8–10). Now *that's* overcoming!

We dare not miss one additional benefit from present sufferings. They make us more desirous of heaven. This is not escapism. Provided we keep sight of today's responsibilities here to God and others, to long for heaven is both healthy and scriptural. It is no more unnatural than a soldier stationed in a war zone who longs to be home. He stays at his post because he was stationed there by his commander. But his heart is back home. Just so, the Christian is often placed on assignment in less-than-desirable conditions by the commander in chief. But his heart is in another place—his true home where pain, suffering, and war do not exist.

IS MY FAITH WEAK?

If a believer who has prayed for healing remains infirm, God is not the culprit. But the question that haunts most Christians who are sick isn't whether or not God has failed. They love and know Him well enough to know that it is impossible for Him to fail. The question that plagues Christians with a lingering malady is whether or not they have failed.

"Perhaps there is sin in my life, and that's why I'm not healed," the believer reasons. Yet if we follow this train of thought, no one could be either healed or saved. It is precisely because we *have* sinned that we need a Savior. God's grace brings us salvation. We didn't earn it. We don't deserve it. It follows that every transaction between God and people is based on God's grace, not the individual's performance. He saves—and heals—not because we are good but because He is good.

"But," the distressed believer continues to probe, "maybe my level of faith wasn't strong enough to be healed." But then we place "faith in God" in two categories: saving faith and healing faith. We believe we have sufficient faith to trust Christ for salvation but somehow lack sufficient faith to trust Him for healing. This is an unscriptural dichotomy. To be saved, one must place his total faith in the power of Jesus Christ to save him. And to be healed, one must do the same thing. Here many believers battle confusion, for they see no difference between the level of faith they exercised for their salvation and the level of faith they are exercising for their healing. Yet, while their sins are forgiven and gone, their sickness remains. There must be something more involved than a lack of faith.

First Things First

There are many roots of sickness and disease, and I believe that a lack of faith for healing can be one reason for continuing illness—but only one. Clearly other dynamics are often involved.

Most prominent are physical roots to sickness that have nothing to do with one's faith or lack of it. To illustrate, many illnesses can be traced to the root causes of obesity and worry. These two conditions are not cured by the prayer of faith. They are cured by repentance and commensurate acts of obedience.

A woman may stand in a healing line expecting deliverance from high blood pressure. If, however, the high blood pressure is caused by hypertension, which in turn is caused by worry, the first step for the woman is not faith for healing but repentance from the sin of worry. Then faith does come into play. She must then learn to trust Jesus Christ fully for all of life's stresses. Then her faith will truly make her whole.

A man may request prayer for healing from heart disease. But if he is sixty pounds overweight, the antidote once again is not faith but repentance. Having brought his eating habits under the lordship of Christ, he can then have unhindered faith for healing because his conscience will no longer condemn him.

Then there are the tougher questions with far more elusive answers. Why was David Watson, an anointed leader in the British renewal, stricken with cancer? Why was he allowed to linger and suffer before eventually succumbing to death? Why did John Wimber die of cancer after bringing so many others into the truths of divine healing? Why were religious but heartless people allowed to mock the "healer" who died? (As if, like the scoffers at the cross, they said: "He healed others, Himself he cannot heal.") Why did my own father, the most godly man I ever knew, die a seemingly premature death at age forty-four?

God will give us answers—answers that will fully satisfy. In the meantime, we should not pray weak prayers of acquiescence—"Lord, if it be Your will, heal this person." Jesus taught us to pray that God's will be done on Earth as in heaven. There is no one sick in heaven, so that is also His will for people on Earth. Until we get to heaven and receive all the answers to things that puzzle us here, we are currently only authorized to pray in faith for healing now.

THE REST OF THE STORY

One could take an entire book to postulate "answers" to such questions. And at best our hypotheses would be conjectural and incomplete. This much we know—our world is imperfect, tainted with sin and its effects, including disease and death. Christ's kingdom has come in our hearts, but it is not yet fully manifested on Earth. Yes, we have seen great and mighty things. We have witnessed miracles. I have seen the crippled walk, the deaf rejoice in restored hearing, the blind see.

Yet some unanswered questions will remain until we see Jesus. To those unanswered questions we must acknowledge an element of mystery: we know only in part. Yet it is precisely this element of mystery that makes God transcendent. His ways are beyond ours: "'For my thoughts are not your thoughts, nor are your ways My ways,' says the LORD. 'For as the heavens are higher than the earth, so are My ways higher than your ways, and My thoughts than your thoughts'" (Isa. 55:8–9). "Who has directed the Spirit of the LORD, or as His counselor has taught Him?" (Isa. 40:13).

There are some of His ways that we may question but that He is not obligated to answer. At least not now. He is God. Period. For this reason, some of His actions regarding us can only be termed mysterious. Yet all are birthed in infinite love.

The ways of almighty God are sometimes complex and mysterious. We insult His holy, omnipotent character when we reduce His options to our wishes. If we put the right amount of money into a soft drink machine, we expect to receive a soft drink. But the analogy cannot be carried over that if we merely make the right confession or believe at the right level we will automatically get what we want. For unlike the soda machine, God is neither mindless nor mechanical. He is omniscient and personal. And while God is never irrational, He is not rationalistic. Sometimes His ways transcend our ability to reason. We cannot be so intellectually arrogant as to remove all mystery from God's ways. As Francis Schaeffer observed, we can know God truly, but, this side of eternity, we cannot know Him fully. What aspects we do know of Him we can know in truth. But it will take an eternity of ever-growing intimacy with Him to fully comprehend His ways. We do get one massive hint right now—*all* His ways flow from His love for us.

We must also take into account the fact that our bodies are not yet redeemed. God's redemptive process begins in the spirit and works progressively outward. At conversion we are saved from the penalty of sin—that is, eternal separation from God. As we yield to the Holy Spirit, we are saved from the power of sin as the soul (comprised of mind, emotions, and will) comes under the lordship of Christ. Ultimately, we will be saved from the very presence of sin. Then the deadly effects of sin will be reversed and our bodies will be raised incorruptible (1 Cor. 15:52).

Every now and then the miniheresy that we have already received our glorified bodies crops up. This teaching is based on a misunderstanding of Christ's promise in John 11:26 that those who believe in Him will never die. This aberrant teaching says that we will never die physically. The truth is that those who know Christ will never die spiritually. But this false teaching asserts that if you believe strongly enough, you will never experience physical death. There is no correlating support for this in Scripture. But when I was growing up, a pastor's wife in our town had fallen prey to this doctrine. Her husband challenged her. "So you already have your glorified body?" he asked. "I'm convinced of it," she retorted. He looked straight into her magnified eyes. "Then why are you wearing those glasses?"

The Bible clearly teaches that we are still "eagerly waiting for the adoption, the redemption of our body" (Rom. 8:23). The body remains under the curse of sin though the spirit has been delivered through the new birth. "Even though our outward man is perishing, yet the inward man is being renewed day by day" (2 Cor. 4:16).

While the believer may wrestle to understand a healing that is delayed, healing for the believer in Jesus is never denied. "By his wounds we are healed" (Isa. 53:5, NIV). That is irrefutable. Many are healed immediately. Others are healed over a period of time. All Christians are forever healed in the resurrection of their bodies. If we keep an eternal perspective, we can look forward to that.

Even the believer who faces terminal illness need never be afraid. Jesus Himself knows what it feels like to die. And He declared, "Because I live, you will live also" (John 14:19).

Until death, the believer trusts the stripes of Jesus for healing. But if death comes, then through and past death the believer continues to trust the blood of Christ. "By His wounds we are healed." Healing will come.

CHAPTER SIX

DEATH'S DEMISE

As long as we are in these bodies, we are away from the Lord. But we live by faith, not by what we see. We should be cheerful, because we would rather leave these bodies and be at home with the Lord. But whether we are at home with the Lord or away from him, we still try our best to please him.

—2 Corinthians 5:6–9, cev

Earth has no sorrow that heaven cannot heal.

—Sir Thomas Moore

After her examination, Dr. Judson asked Mrs. Thompson to be seated in his office. He chose his words carefully. "I want to be completely honest with you, Mrs. Thompson." He paused and drew an extended breath. "We've discovered cancer in advanced stages throughout your body. We will treat it as best we can. But barring a miracle, your days are numbered."

Mrs. Thompson's life seemed to flash before her. In a few seconds' time she sped through the emotional roller coaster of shock, disbelief, numbness, anger, and fear. Then a familiar peace steadied her dizzying ride.

"Dr. Judson," she began, "you say my days are numbered." Wiping her tears and looking up with a smile, she announced, "Well, doctor, so are yours."

The Bible teaches emphatically that each of us has an allotted time on Earth, time enough (however brief it may seem) to recognize our need for a Savior, our need for Jesus Christ. Sadly, not everyone comes to this conclusion, thinking instead that he or she has found another "comparable" answer.

The fact that we live in an age baptized in relativism was brought home to me forcibly as I was sharing my faith in Christ with a man seated next to me on a plane. After listening patiently to my presentation of the gospel, he replied, "That may be the truth for you but not for me. I have another truth."

Another truth! A generation of situation ethics has produced a postmodern era where truth itself is perceived as relative. This was also graphically portrayed by the young man who commented to me, "I don't have to worry about hell. I don't believe in it." My reply to him was that no amount of belief or disbelief in hell would make it disappear. The fact remains.

In the same way, many people form theories about death based on their wishes instead of facts. Yet the Bible gives clear facts concerning death. Since death is sure for everyone (barring the return of Christ for His church), wisdom cries that we prepare for this inevitable event.

THREE FACTS ABOUT DEATH

A single verse of Scripture gives a concise overview of the Bible's teaching on death. Hebrews 9:27 says, "It is appointed for men to die once, but after this the judgment."

From this passage three important facts emerge concerning death. First, death happens once. "It is appointed for men to die *once*..." The only time in which to invest for eternity is now, in this life. The current fad of belief in reincarnation is but one more tragic deception. Whether one buys into this aberration of reality by way of a contemporary spirituality or an ancient religious system, the fact remains that people die once, not many times. Reservations for heaven must be made in this life, for this is the only one there is. How ironic that an old beer commercial contains more theological truth than some religious fads: "You only go around once in life!"

Second, death is not a termination, nor is it entrance into "soul sleep," as some believe. Rather, it is a momentary interruption in an ongoing life. Death merely transfers us out of one sphere of existence into another. But life itself goes on. "It is appointed for men to die once, but *after this...*"

Third, death is followed by judgment. "It is appointed for men to die once, but after this *the judgment.*" The theory of universal salvation is rejected by this scripture. The unrepentant will face judgment and eternity without Christ.

A good summary of what the Bible teaches regarding this vital subject is found in the Westminster Confession:

1. The bodies of men, after death, return to dust, and see corruption; but their souls (which neither die nor sleep), having an immortal subsistence, immediately return to God who gave them. The souls of the righteous, being then made perfect in holiness, are received into the highest heavens, where they behold the face of God in light and glory, waiting for the full redemption of their bodies; and the souls of the wicked are cast into hell, where they remain in torments and utter darkness, reserved to the judgment of the great day. Besides these two places for souls separated from their bodies, the Scripture acknowledgeth none.

2. At the last day, such as are found alive shall not die, but be changed; and all the dead shall be raised up with the selfsame bodies, and none other, although with different

qualities, which shall be united again to their souls forever.[1]

These points are in keeping with Scripture and provide solid pillars of truth for our future. How different from the story I heard of a friend of a deceased atheist who came to the funeral home to pay his respects. As he looked at the corpse of his friend, he shook his head and said, "Poor Bob. He's all dressed up with no place to go."

But the Bible teaches that the unrepentant do indeed have somewhere to go: a place of torment "where their worm does not die, and the fire is not quenched" (Mark 9:48). This alternative to heaven is the eternal dwelling of those who reject the forgiveness offered in Jesus Christ. John Milton described it in his epic *Paradise Lost*:

> A Dungeon horrible on all sides round,
> As one great Furnace flam'd, yet from those flames
> No light, but rather darkness visible
> Serv'd only to discover sights of woe
> Regions of sorrow, doleful shades, where peace
> And rest can never dwell, hope never comes
> That comes to all; but torture without end.[2]

The Christian and Death

As a minister, I probably attend more funerals than most people. And I can tell you this. There is as much difference between the attitudes of Christians and unbelievers toward death as there is between light and darkness, between heaven and hell.

For the non-Christian, death is a destroyer. But for the Christian, death is a door. For the non-Christian, death is a deceiver. But for the Christian, death is a deliverance. Freed from the body's earthbound limitations, the transported Christian enters a realm where there are no limits.

Paul understood this when he wrote both to the Corinthian and

Philippian churches that his preference would be to already be in heaven.[3] Understanding, however, that his race was not yet completed, he determined to stay faithful and fruitful until the glad day that he went home to be with the Lord. Paul also knew that the entire church—past and those present on Earth at the Lord's return—would be reunited around the One they adore. "I can tell you this directly from the Lord," he wrote. "We who are still living when the Lord returns will not rise to meet him ahead of those who are in their graves. For the Lord himself will come down from heaven with a commanding shout, with the call of the archangel, and with the trumpet call of God. First, all the Christians who have died will rise from their graves. Then, together with them, we who are still alive and remain on the earth will be caught up in the clouds to meet the Lord in the air and remain with him forever. So comfort and encourage each other with these words" (1 Thess. 4:15–17, NLT).

So when confronted with death, Christians smile through their tears. Why? Because they know that the angel of death does not get the last word; death—though a vicious enemy—does not win. Christians face the raw, coarse realities of death, feeling all its chilling effects, and still land safely on the other side.

In 1852 Vermont pastor Daniel Jackson wrote this obituary for his wife, Mary, who had suffered from a long illness:

> The triumphant state of her mind softened every agony, hushed every murmur, and completely disarmed the king of terrors. For awhile, she had a sharp conflict with the power of attachment which bound her to family and friends, but by the grace of God she obtained a glorious victory and longed to depart and be with Christ, which is far better.
>
> I will here notice some of her dying words uttered during the last week of her life. Speaking of the happy state into which she was about to enter, she exclaimed, "O glorious day, O blessed hope, my heart leaps forward at the thought." When distressed for breath, she would say, "Blessed Jesus, receive my spirit." When I spoke to her about her

thirst, she said, "When I have been thirsty I have thought of that river whose streams make glad the city of God."[4]

Scripture tells us that "the path of the just is like the shining sun, that shines ever brighter unto the perfect day" (Prov. 4:18). The Christian knows that death ushers him immediately into the secure presence of Jesus. And the believer longs for and anticipates this home going.

How wonderfully different from the general prescription society gives for dealing with death. It drugs the dying until death, then drugs the living to make it through the funeral. It seems significant that Jesus refused to take the pain-killing drink offered Him while He was dying. Instead of numbing reality, He chose to taste the undiluted bile of death for Himself and for every person (Heb. 2:9). Of course, I am *not* saying that Christians should deny themselves medications when needed. I am saying that we are able, by faith in Jesus Christ, to take the worst death can dish out and still come away victorious. David Watson wrote, "The church is the only society on earth that never loses a member through death! As a Christian I believe not just in life *after* death, but in life *through* death."[5] And Erwin Lutzer wrote in *One Minute After You Die,* "While your family tends to your funeral you are beholding the face of Christ. Though the family weeps at your departure, you would not return to earth even if the choice were given to you. Having seen heaven, you will find that earth has lost all its attraction."[6]

For the follower of Jesus the future is always better and brighter, even though death is part of the future. Such an assurance should make the believer both a realist and an optimist, no matter what the current crisis. Whatever comes, death or life, Jesus is first and Jesus is King. "For if we live, we live to the Lord; and if we die, we die to the Lord. Therefore, whether we live or die, we are the Lord's" (Rom. 14:8).

Some Christians today seem to think that dying would be evidence of some spiritual lack. They're praying for the Lord to return before they die. Of course, all of us should have hearts filled with expectancy concerning Christ's return. But do such statements sometimes belie a fear of death? Charles Spurgeon, London's great preacher of the late 1800s, said he actually looked forward to dying. "What could be more sacred than the experience of dying in Jesus?" he asked. Spurgeon believed the death of a Christian to be the ultimate Christian experience. Just imagine what it will be like to be personally escorted from this world to the next by Jesus Christ!

In fact, the Christian never tastes the full dregs of death. Jesus Christ has done that for us. Jesus said that the one who believes in Him will never die. And it's true—though our physical bodies will one day cease to function, we will escape death's full effects. Having left the earthly sphere, we will be instantly in the presence of the Lord. Life is interrupted but not terminated. As D. L. Moody once said, "Soon you will read in the newspaper that I am dead. Don't believe it for a moment. I will be more alive than ever before."

An aged Christian lay on her deathbed, just a few hours away from eternity. Her pastor came to comfort her. "Young man," she said with a confident smile, "I have no fear coming to this river of death. My Father owns the land on both sides of the river. I'm just transferring to His land on the other side."

This longing for a permanent home, far from producing morbid pessimists, has an extremely healthy effect on our lives here and now. This is not a death wish. Rather, it is a *life wish*, a desire to be with the Lord. Vance Havner, a renowned preacher, is now home with the Lord. He not only lived but also preached until he was almost ninety. He often mentioned, comically yet truthfully, "The hope of death is what's kept me alive so long!"

I believe the death of the righteous has an illustrative counterpart in nature. In my first pastorate, while I was in college in Arkansas, I would drive through the Ozarks in the fall of the year, reveling in the beauty of God's creation and communing with Him. I knew the leaves would be cold and dead in a few weeks. But at that point, just before death, they were ablaze with spectacular color.

This visual aid reminds us that the greatest brilliance in a believer's life, spiritually and otherwise, is often just prior to death. This display of color and life is a final testimony on this earth that our mighty God is also faithful. This covenant-keeping God has promised that His faithfulness extends as long as there is seedtime and harvest, winter and summer, as long as there are seasons (Gen. 8:22). No wonder the Bible says, "Precious in the sight of the LORD is the death of His saints" (Ps. 116:15). Even in the process of dying, a unique beauty unfolds. And through it the Christian gives striking testimony to the faithfulness of his God.

WHEN LOVED ONES DIE

The confidence that we are redemptively connected to the never-ending life of Christ steadies us through any crisis. Because of this assurance in Jesus, we can not only face the prospects of our own deaths, but we can also get up off the bed of grief and live again after the death of a loved one.

When I was fifteen, my father died. Along with my mother and sisters, I went through months of stinging heartache and unanswered questions. But I was never without the assurance of God's presence. And one morning, several months after my dad's death, I woke with the acute awareness of birds singing outside my window. While the pain was still there, cool, refreshing gushes of hope ran over my soul. I knew, in spite of our loss, we had a future.

For the trusting believer, no matter how dark the night, *morning always follows mourning.* "Weeping may endure for a night, but joy comes in the morning" (Ps. 30:5). For the unbeliever, life itself is in the process of unwinding. But not so for the Christian. After the cross, the resurrection. After night, day. After death, life. After despair, hope. Man's time cycles start with light and end with night, but God's pattern is the inverse: "The evening and the morning were the first day." Notice the sequence. Always with Him the best is yet to be.

It's impossible to describe fully the inner peace of Christ's comfort during grief. Perhaps it can only be illustrated. One well-known story that tenderly illustrates this divine aid is the story of Horatio G. Spafford. Mr. Spafford was a successful Chicago lawyer who enjoyed a close friendship with D. L. Moody, Ira Sankey, and several other evangelical leaders of his day. In 1873, on the advice of their family physician and for his wife's health, he planned a European trip for his family. At the last minute, Spafford was unable to accompany his wife and four daughters due to late business developments. So while Mr. Spafford stayed in Chicago, he sent his family ahead, as scheduled, on the S.S. *Ville du Havre* in November 1873. He anticipated joining them in a few days.

On November 22, the *Ville du Havre* was struck by the *Lochearn*, an English ship, and sank twelve minutes later. Though Mrs. Spafford was saved from the icy Atlantic, all four daughters perished. On December 1, the survivors landed at Cardiff, Wales. Mrs. Spafford cabled her husband, "Saved alone."

Quickly, a brokenhearted Spafford left Chicago to join his grieving wife. On the high seas, near the scene of the tragedy, he wrote this hymn:

> When peace, like a river, attendeth my way,
> When sorrows like sea billows roll;
> Whatever my lot, Thou hast taught me to say,
> "It is well, it is well with my soul."
>
> Though Satan should buffet, though trials should come,
> Let this blest assurance control,
> That Christ has regarded my helpless estate,
> And hath shed His own blood for my soul.
>
> And, Lord, haste the day when the faith shall be sight,
> The clouds be rolled back as a scroll,
> The trump shall resound and the Lord shall descend,
> "Even so," it is well with my soul.[7]

This prospect of a glad reunion at the feet of Jesus has buttressed the hopes of millions through the centuries. Death is never the final word.

LASTING INFLUENCE

Paul was able to come to the end of his life and announce to his longtime friend Timothy, "For I am already being poured out as a drink offering, and the time of my departure is at hand. I have fought the good fight, I have finished the race, I have kept the faith" (2 Tim. 4:6–7). In essence he was saying, "I have accomplished God's will for my life." In the face of death nothing is more reassuring than that. Success in life is simply to know the will of God and to do it. Paul was beaten, spat on, and shipwrecked. Some think his wife deserted him. He was verbally abused. Fellow Christians impugned his motives. But his life was a success. He knew God's will for him—and did it.

Some time ago I stood in the small room in John Wesley's house in London where he died. Having lived almost ninety years he turned the tide of a decadent nation and was the catalyst for spiritual renewal. Even some secular historians attribute him with saving England from the kind of bloodbath that was drenching France. Wesley's last words, shortly before he drifted into eternity, were, "The best of all is, God is with us!"

David Brainerd's short life of piety left a lasting impression on the church. His life of prayer and missionary passion remains a model of courage. Dying at Northampton on October 9, 1747, some of his final words were: "I am almost in eternity; I long to be there. My work is done. I have done with my friends—all the world is nothing to me. Oh, to be in Heaven to praise and glorify God with His holy angels!"

When we think of Charles Dickens, we usually think of his legacy of classic books like *Oliver Twist, David Copperfield,* and *A Christmas Carol.* But his most lasting legacy is the inheritance recorded in his will. He wrote, "I commit my soul to the mercy of God, through our Lord and Savior Jesus Christ, and I exhort my dear children humbly to try and guide themselves by the teaching of the New Testament."[8]

My own father retained confidence in Jesus to the end of his life. His influence reached many nations as he led the church he pastored in giving 50 percent of its income to world missions, from the first offering they ever received until his death ten years later. As he was dying, he looked at the attending nurse in the hospital and smiled. "Good-bye," he said. "Thank You, Jesus." With that, he was transported to heaven.

We live in the time prophesied by Scripture when men's hearts would fail them for fear (Luke 21:26). But for the Christian, even death is teeming with hope. "So when this corruptible has put on incorruption, and this mortal has put on immortality, then shall be brought to pass the saying that is written: 'Death is swallowed up in victory.' 'O Death, where is your sting? O Hades, where is your victory?' The sting of death is sin, and the strength of sin is the law. But thanks be to God, who gives us the victory through our Lord Jesus Christ" (1 Cor. 15:54–57).

In a paranoid world we can live and die with confidence. Jesus has taken the sting out of death.

CHAPTER SEVEN

THE CHEMISTRY
OF THE UNIVERSE

You know that those who are considered rulers over the Gentiles lord it over them, and their great ones exercise authority over them. Yet it shall not be so among you, but whoever desires to become great among you shall be your servant. And whoever of you desires to be first shall be slave of all. For even the Son of Man did not come to be served, but to serve, and to give His life a ransom for many.

—MARK 10:42–45

Consider humility to be indeed the mother virtue, your very first duty before God, the one perpetual safeguard of the soul.[1]

—ANDREW MURRAY

YOU MAY REMEMBER THE OLD STORY OF HOW SIR WALTER RALEIGH threw his cloak over a muddy puddle, making it a carpet for the queen to walk on. His action was heralded as a selfless act of chivalry. How noble that he would forgo his expensive cloak for the good of the crown! But Sir Walter was nobody's fool. He knew that nothing is ever really lost that is laid down for royalty. And when he organized expeditions to the New World, he did not lack a powerful backer for his ventures.

In the same way, those things we lay down for Jesus Christ are never truly lost. Fortunes may be laid down. Plans and dreams may be surrendered. Even lives may be sacrificed. But they are never lost. There is always an overwhelming compensation for anything we give to Him. God will be in no person's debt. That which is laid down for His majesty will be generously recompensed both in this life and on that day. And the more unselfishly we give, the more we become like Jesus.

St. Francis of Assisi understood this well. In a time of opulent indulgence in the church, he took a voluntary vow of poverty. His simple lifestyle and innocent devotion to Christ were powerful rebukes to the greed that had engulfed Christendom. In his famous prayer to be an instrument of God's peace, St. Francis makes this observation: "It is in giving that we receive. It is in pardoning that we are pardoned. It is in dying that we are born to eternal life." In God's inverted scheme of things, those who win by intimidation lose everything, and those who lose by self-sacrifice win it all.

HUMILITY'S ATTITUDE

In the second chapter of Philippians Paul graphically details how Jesus emptied Himself of His prerogatives as God. And Paul says we are to pour out our lives as well. "Your attitude [of humility and service] should be the same as that of Christ Jesus," he tells us (Phil. 2:5, NIV).

A beautiful picture of this is seen in the old covenant drink offering. Once, during a battle in which the Philistines occupied Bethlehem, King David made an off-the-cuff remark that some water from the well near Bethlehem's gate would sure taste good in the heat of that battle. The trouble was, that well was behind enemy lines. Yet three of his mighty men immediately put their lives at risk and retrieved the valued water for their king. Then David did something that at first glance might seem insane. Because the men had risked their lives, "David would not drink it, but poured it out to the LORD" (1 Chron. 11:18). David knew he had an option. He could take that costly commodity—Bethlehem's water—and consume it on himself. If he chose to do this, no one would have complained. After all, David needed that water for his sustenance.

Or he could choose to surrender the blessing that had come to him at great cost as a costly offering to the Lord. David chose the latter. Later he remarked, "Nor will I offer...offerings to the LORD my God with that which costs me nothing" (2 Sam. 24:24).

In the same way, your life is valuable. You have the choice to indulge yourself or pour your life out as a drink offering to the Lord. But once again, that which is poured out is not lost. The costly offering is stored up in another world as an eternally valuable treasure for you in heaven.

Paul warned of a self-absorbed generation that would emerge in the last days: "People will be lovers of themselves, lovers of money, boastful, proud, abusive, disobedient to parents, ungrateful, unholy, without love, unforgiving, slanderous, without self-control, brutal, not lovers of the good, treacherous, rash, conceited, lovers of pleasure rather than lovers of God—having a form of godliness but denying its power" (2 Tim. 3:2–5, NIV). Was he reading this morning's newspaper? It sure sounds like it. His description is on target in describing our society.

To speak of laying down our lives, emptying and pouring them out, sounds shrill and alien, even to the ears of many contemporary Christians. We've been conditioned even in our walk with the Lord to ask, "What's in it for me?" We have been told that ours is a faith of receiving. And, of course, this is wonderfully true. I am not denying any of the rich benefits of our new covenant in Christ. But there are two sides to this coin. All Christianity is a life of receiving. But mature Christianity is also a life of sacrificial giving.

It is a distinct privilege for me to serve Christ and His Great Commission alongside some of the greatest men and women alive today. They are leaders of the church in the poorer, developing nations of our world. These brothers and sisters have taught me much about true, Christ-honoring humility. They represent a new model of Christian leadership emerging for this new century. These believers possess anointing without arrogance, boldness without brashness, and power without pride. They display the kind of God-honoring leadership Fred Smith Sr. had in mind when he said, "Humility is not denying the power you have. It is realizing that the power comes through you, not from you."[2]

After persecuting the church before his conversion, Paul spent the rest of his life pouring out every ounce of energy and influence for the church and the advance of the gospel. Concerning his schedule that never let up, he commented, "If I am being poured out as a drink offering on the sacrifice and service of your faith, I am glad and rejoice with you all" (Phil. 2:17).

Paul had just rehearsed how Jesus Himself was the prime example of what it means to be poured out. But because of His giving of Himself—from heaven to a manger to a cross—"God also has highly exalted Him and given Him the name which is above every name, that at the name of Jesus every knee should bow, of those in heaven, and of those on earth, and of those under the earth, and that every tongue should confess that Jesus Christ is Lord, to the glory of God the Father" (Phil. 2:9–11).

The chemistry of the universe has taken effect. Humbling has brought exaltation.

Self-Worth and the Gospel

Both James and Peter exhort us to voluntarily humble ourselves before the Lord so He can exalt us at the proper time. They also warn us that God sets Himself against the proud.[3] Yet many people today are so insecure they fear any self-sacrifice. And people are as individual as snowflakes and every bit as fragile. Often they feel that their worth would be jeopardized by placing themselves in a vulnerable position of servanthood. Servants, after all, can be stepped on, despised, or, worse yet, ignored.

But it should be remembered that our intrinsic worth as humans has nothing to do with status. The emaciated Somalian child is just as valuable as the head of a major corporation. The hunchbacked Indian who sweeps the floor all day with a whisk broom is just as valuable as the most glamorous Hollywood movie star. Some may not really believe that, but God does. And it's His opinion that matters.

Communism was dehumanizing because it denied that people are made in the image of God. Dostoyevsky's warning proved tragically prophetic: "Without God, everything is permitted." But capitalistic materialism also has its dehumanizing effects. We may laugh at the stilted syntax of the teenage girl who says, "See, like, there's this guy, and, well, like, he drives a Jag." But ultimately it portrays a disturbing inability in our society to separate person from possessions. People, no matter what they possess or do not possess, are of infinite value. In fact, people are so valuable that heaven dispatched its greatest Prize to bring these erring earthlings eternally home. I love the way John 3:16 begins in the Amplified Version: "For God so greatly loved and dearly prized the world that He [even] gave up His only begotten (unique) Son..." And whether or not these humans are physically attractive, they are beautiful. Some of our simplest children's songs are also simply profound: "Red and yellow, black and white, they are precious in His sight."[4]

Your value as a person is based on three important truths. *First, you are valuable because you are made in the image of God.* Like God, you can think, choose, and create. You also have the capacity to know God and love Him. Because we all carry the image of our Creator, each person is infinitely precious. Consequently all human life is to be cherished and protected from conception until death.

Respect for all humans is based on this important theological fact—all people are created in God's image. This separates and elevates us above all the rest of God's creation. "If I see myself as one more species of animal, with no life beyond this one and no accountability to a Higher Power, then why not follow the pleasure instinct to the end?" Philip Yancey asks. "On the other hand, if I see this planet as God's world, and my longings as rumors of another world, then I want to connect those clues to God's overall plan. I want to bring the two worlds together, and I do so by accepting that we human beings must look beyond ourselves—above ourselves—in ordering our desires."[5]

Second, you are valuable because of the price paid for your redemption. As Bonhoeffer said, "God's grace is free, but it is not cheap." If ever you doubt your worth, look again at Calvary. And if ever you doubt that God loves you, look again at the dying Man on that cross. It is conceptually true that Jesus died for the world. But it is personally true that He died for you. His death touches you at the point of your need for love, acceptance, and forgiveness.

Third, you are valuable because of the unique contribution only you can make to the human experience. There is a circle of people you can reach that no one else can reach. No one can touch them quite like you. There may be a book in you no one else can write, a song no one else can compose, an affirmation no one else can offer, a discovery no one else can make. It belongs uniquely to you. And if you don't deliver, we will all be the poorer for it. God made you to be the world's best at something. Find out what that something is and pursue it to the glory of God.

When these three simple truths become actual revelations inside you, you will have a foundation for inner security. Any identity crisis will be a thing of the past. Then you will be able to build on that foundation to even greater security as you discover more fully who you are in Christ. Augustine observed, "If you plan to build a house of virtues, you must first lay deep foundations of humility."

Only the secure risk voluntary servitude. Yet only those who serve are truly fulfilled. Richard Foster wrote, "Of all the classic Spiritual Disciplines, service is the most conducive to the growth of humility. When we set out on a consciously chosen course of action that accents the good of others and is, for the most part, a hidden work, a deep change occurs in our spirits."[6]

Many serve behind the scenes so those on the front lines are free to give themselves to the battle. Most people cry at weddings. I tend to get misty-eyed at graduations. Think of the sacrifices parents, spouses, and children have made to see their loved one in a cap and gown. And one day every faithful worker and trustworthy behind-the-scenes person will share in the reward of the ones out front. The Bible promises, "The share of the man who stayed with the supplies is to be the same as that of him who went down to the battle. All will share alike" (1 Sam. 30:24, NIV).

Charles Spurgeon wrote, "Seek secrecy for your good deeds. Do not even see your own virtue. Hide from yourself that which you yourself have done that is commendable; for the proud contemplation of your own generosity may tarnish all your alms. Keep the thing so secret that even you yourself are hardly aware that you are doing anything at all praiseworthy. Let God be present, and you will have enough of an audience. He will reward you, reward you 'openly,' reward you as a Father rewards a child, reward you as one who saw what you did, and knew that you did it wholly unto Him."[7]

PROMOTION'S SOURCE

The Bible says, "Exaltation comes neither from the east nor from the west nor from the south. But God is the Judge: He puts down one, and exalts another" (Ps. 75:6–7). Contrary to what many believe, promotion is not a matter of being in the right place at the right time so the right guy can give you a break. Promotion comes from the Lord. And He always delights in lifting pure-hearted servants. "For the eyes of the Lord range throughout the earth to strengthen those whose hearts are fully committed to him" (2 Chron. 16:9, NIV).

Yet the servant who realizes the dignity of his calling isn't really looking for promotion. He is looking for the Lord's nod of approval on his present assignment; that's all. He is content where he is, realizing that it is the Lord who has put him there. Andrew Murray had a deeper perception of servanthood than most. He said, "When we see that humility is something infinitely deeper than contrition, and accept it as our participation in the life of Jesus, we will begin to learn that it is our true nobility, and that to prove it in being servants of all is the highest fulfillment of our destiny, as men created in the image of God."[8]

Someone said that real humility is not thinking more of yourself than you should, nor thinking less of yourself than you should. In short, humility is not thinking of yourself. This is what Dietrich Bonhoeffer meant when he wrote, "To be called to a life of extraordinary quality, to live up to it, and yet to be unconscious of it is indeed a narrow way."[9] It is the narrow way to which Christ calls us.[10]

To allow the life of Christ to flow through our lives is the zenith of dignity. And when we allow His life to flow through ours, servanthood is the inevitable result. This is genuine success, to live in heaven's honor. It's the kind of self-sacrifice some believers voluntarily opted for in the firm confidence that there was a great payoff for their sacrifice:

> All these people were still living by faith when they died. They did not receive the things promised; they only saw them and welcomed them from a distance. And they admitted that they were aliens and strangers on earth. People who say such things show that they are looking for a country of their own.... they were longing for a better country—a heavenly one. Therefore God is not ashamed to be called their God, for he has prepared a city for them.
>
> —HEBREWS 11:13–16, NIV

Paul Rees wrote, "If you want a picture of success as heaven measures it, of greatness as God views it, don't look for the blaring of the bands on Broadway; listen, rather, for the tinkle of water splashing into a basin, while God incarnate, in a humility that makes angels hold their breath, sponges the grime from the feet of His undeserving disciples."[11]

After Jesus performed this astonishing act, He endured the even greater indignity and demotion of being stripped, tortured, and cruelly executed. But, little known to His human enemies or to Satan, He was only hours away from ransacking hell of its captives and rising as the almighty Lord of life. His final step up was to the Father's right hand, "angels and authorities and powers having been made subject to Him" (1 Pet. 3:22).

Now we are called to follow in His steps of humility and servant-hood. But, having done so, we will also follow in His cycle of victory and exaltation. It's the chemistry of the universe.

CHAPTER EIGHT

Is That Your Final Answer?

The day will surely come when God, by Jesus Christ, will judge everyone's secret life. This is my message.

—Romans 2:16, nlt

The most important thought I ever had was that of my individual responsibility to God.

—Daniel Webster

SOME TIME AGO DURING AN INTERVIEW WITH *Ministry Today* magazine I was asked, "What will be a marked difference in ministering in the twenty-first century?" I replied, "Trust will be harder to gain and easier to lose." Recent revelations have only underscored this sobering truth.

I'm writing this chapter in the aftermath of one of the most egregious scandals in modern church history. Almost all the Christians I've talked with say the news of this beloved minister's fall felt much like a slug to the stomach with a baseball bat. God help us if we do not learn from this. God help us if we do not change from this.

The past several years have been rough for high-visibility ministers. Close scrutiny from both friends and foes has uncovered lurid revelations of immorality, infighting, and greed. Heartbroken Christians together with outside critics are asking, "What's wrong with this picture? What's going on in the church? How could this ever have happened?" When I was getting my teeth cleaned, the dental assistant spoke for many when she asked me, "Isn't there *anybody* out there who's above reproach anymore?"

One conclusion everyone has come to is that no one is perfect. Of course, this is no grand revelation. It is merely a reiteration of Scripture's age-old teaching that all have sinned.[1] But we must be careful not to take this admission too far. Instead of repenting of our sins and drawing on God's grace to live holy lives, we seem to use our imperfection as an excuse for indiscretion.

What *has* happened to us? Where did we begin to lose our grip on just plain decency? At what point did the moral downturn become a moral freefall? One shift in focus needs to be noted in particular. For the last several years we have tended to embrace a no-accountability gospel. Sometimes it was preached in outright statements. At other times it was just inferred, sort of a Christianized version of "Don't worry. Be happy." It came out sounding something like this: "Jesus has forgiven you. That 'conviction' you feel isn't from God. Your sins are covered. We live under grace." We *do* live under grace, and (if we're truly born again) our sins *are* covered. That is wonderfully true. But the implied message was, "Therefore we have no further accountability to God." And that is blatantly false.

If we rightly understand God's grace, we will live holy lives. True grace has a didactic effect—it teaches us to honor God, live for His glory, and look toward our future with Him. "For the grace of God that brings salvation has appeared to all men. It teaches us to say 'No' to ungodliness and worldly passions, and to live self-controlled, upright and godly lives in this present age, while we wait for the blessed hope— the glorious appearing of our great God and Savior, Jesus Christ" (Titus 2:11–13, NIV).

But the "dis-graceful" message of some of our leaders was a not-so-subtle suggestion that, since they were anointed and chosen above the masses, God had somehow struck a special deal with them. God would cut them a little more slack since His hand of blessing was on them. And before we become angry at that kind of twisted thinking, remember that good-hearted men like Samson, Saul, and David all bought into it. Far from getting off more lightly, James warns aspiring leaders, "We who teach will be judged by God *with greater strictness*" (James 3:1, NLT, emphasis added).

It was this coming accountability to Christ, with an even stricter standard for leaders, that prompted Charles Wesley to write:

> Arm me with jealous care,
> As in Thy sight to live;
> And O Thy servant, Lord, prepare
> A strict account to give.[2]

Clearly, "the time has come for judgment to begin at the house of God" (1 Pet. 4:17). It has begun with a few of our highest-profile leaders being exposed as duplicitous. But before the mockers blast too harshly, let them remember the rest of that verse: "And if it begins with us first, what will be the end of those who do not obey the gospel of God?"

A NEW CALL TO ACCOUNTABILITY

One hesitates to write or preach on accountability, particularly in the present climate. Far better than any critics, I am acutely aware of my own struggles and my constant need to draw on God's enabling grace. I know all too well what can lurk in my own heart. Anyone who would issue a fresh call to holiness feels like saying with Paul, "Who is sufficient for these things?" (2 Cor. 2:16). And the closer we get to God, the brighter the searchlight of His piercing purity. John Wesley, known as the great "holiness preacher," felt keenly his own fallibility. But he also knew that his weaknesses did not cancel out God's truth. So he concluded, "I will preach holiness until I am holy. I will preach sanctification until I am sanctified."

Often I find my heart breathing the prayer of an old hymn:

> O to grace how great a debtor
> Daily I'm constrained to be!
> Let Thy grace, Lord, like a fetter
> Bind my wandr'ing heart to Thee;
> Prone to wander, Lord, I feel it,
> Prone to leave the God I love;
> Here's my heart, Lord, O take and seal it,
> Seal it for Thy courts above.[3]

God is pointedly requiring a new commitment to integrity and a new perception of true success. Charles Malik, former president of the General Assembly of the United Nations, said shortly before he died, "Success is neither fame, wealth nor power; rather it is seeking, knowing, loving and obeying God." Is that the standard of success we're preaching today?

Our unaccountability message has produced unaccountable people. And when people sense they are not accountable, their sin-tainted natures throw off restraints. But Jesus warns us, "There is nothing hidden which will not be revealed, nor has anything been kept secret but that it should come to light" (Mark 4:22). Now, was Jesus speaking metaphorically, or did He actually mean that? And if you were a betting person, how much would you wager against a literal interpretation? If we take what He said at face value (and there is no reason not to), that means nothing hidden or secret will stay that way.

So investigative reporters are the least of our concerns. The Holy Spirit Himself is doing His own investigation. And He will hold us fully accountable. Knowing our own proclivity to sin, we must flee to the Investigator who is also the Exonerator. The same Spirit who brings our sins to light gives us power over them.

"Before Jesus" in Relationships

I love the story a man who is now a respected Christian leader relates of how his mother taught him to tell the truth when he was a little boy. Having stolen cookies from the cookie jar, he tried to hide his guilt. "Son," his mother inquired, "did you take any cookies?" Poker-faced, he replied, "No. I didn't." Then his mother restated the question. "Son, *before Jesus*, did you take any cookies from the jar?" The boy gulped and replied, "Well, if you put it like that, yes, I did."

Everything in our lives is before Jesus. We need to remember that, especially in the area of relationships and all our interactions with people. I am thrilled when I see Christians as the quick first responders to victims of disasters. While others of their own religion seem paralyzed and unable to help their fellow Muslims or fellow Hindus in crisis, Christians quickly come to the aid of any who are suffering, no matter what their religion. But this all goes back to theology. Those other belief systems espouse a religious determinism that says that the "fate" of the victims was the Almighty's punishment, or at least His uncontestable will. The verdict has been pronounced; their lives no longer count. But our faith will never allow us to view anyone anywhere as an expendable object. Rather, Christians believe that all people—even those who oppose the gospel—are created in God's image, and simply because they are humans they are the crowning glory of His creation. Their lives count.

So how should we deal with assaults against us and against our faith? Jesus tells us explicitly how to process painful experiences when we are despised for our allegiance to Him. "Blessed are you when men hate you," Jesus taught, "when they exclude you and insult you and reject your name as evil, because of the Son of Man. Rejoice in that day and leap for joy, because great is your reward in heaven" (Luke 6:22–23, NIV). In fact, it was in reference to people who oppose the kingdom of God that Jesus said everything would one day come to light. Jesus had just been encouraging His disciples to stand firm for Him when they were persecuted. And it was in that context that Jesus said we are never to fear our enemies. "So do not be afraid of them. There is nothing concealed that will not be disclosed, or hidden that will not be made known" (Matt. 10:26, NIV). That means that there is a coming day when God will throw the spotlight of Christ's approval on all who have suffered for Him, especially those who have suffered in secret. That same spotlight will also expose all His enemies and their undercover operations against Him. In our day we seldom hear about many of the atrocities against Christians. The mainline press often seems in unholy collusion with the enemies of the church to conceal cruelties against believers. But one day soon God's spotlight will expose every covert operation against Him and His people.

Corrie ten Boom (who knew something about suffering for righteousness' sake) said, "Every experience God gives us, every person He puts in our lives, is the perfect preparation for the future that only He can see."[4] No one comes into your life by accident. They are there either for you to minister to them or for them to minister to you. Not only that, there is, as Corrie reminded us, some purpose that may be yet unseen that brings lives together.

The concept of acting in a God-honoring way in human relations is perhaps most violated these days in interactions with the opposite sex. This inevitably leads to people being violated. Sadly, in our day there is often little difference between the sexual conduct of Christians and unbelievers. Many who profess faith in Christ have bought into the same fraudulent rationales for permissiveness as unbelievers. Haven't you heard it? "We know it's OK. God knows our hearts. He understands, and He wants us to be happy."

Whose Bible are these people reading? (And that's part of the problem—they're usually not reading the Bible at all.) Not only is this flirting with fire, but it is also courting moral and spiritual disaster. Elisabeth Elliot cogently battles this loose thinking (and loose living):

Christians who are buying such rubbish today are without honor. They have lost the notions of fidelity, renunciation, and sacrifice, because nothing seems worth all that. There is nothing for which they will pay the price of actual, conscious, painful, down-to-earth self-denial—*except* (and I am convinced this is a significant exception) visible gains like money and sports. If young people have heroes today, they are athletes. If they have role models of endurance and sacrifice and self-discipline, they are athletes. If a man denies himself comforts, vacations, pleasures with his family, evenings at home, or the free indulgence of whatever appetite he feels, it is usually for money. Nobody will worry very much about his being repressive or fanatical or weird, so long as money is his motive. If your goal is purity of heart, be prepared to be thought very odd.[5]

Powerful words. There is a visible gain for purity of heart; it just isn't always seen today. But visible, tangible rewards do await the pure.

"Before Jesus" in Stewardship of Money

The Bible clearly commands us not to work merely to become rich: "Do not wear yourself out to get rich; have the wisdom to show restraint" (Prov. 23:4, NIV). Yet vast numbers are racing at breakneck speed as workaholics, trying to secure financially the very families they are losing through overwork. But if we do not work primarily for the purpose of money, why work at all?

One reason is that work itself is honorable. God blesses human labor. Indeed, it can be an act of worship to offer our work to God. We work to the glory of God. In exchange for the investment of our time at work—which really constitutes an investing of our lives—we are given money. What we do with that money is "before Jesus." It is honorable to meet our financial obligations. Failure to do so brings reproach on the name of Christ. It is commendable to invest for the future, give to the needy, make our families secure, and allow money to do what it can do in alleviating suffering, advancing the gospel, and extending God's kingdom. It is not particularly honorable to give a tenth of our incomes back to

God. God does promise to bless us when we tithe, but tithing is simply an understood part of our devotion as serious God-followers. As we obey the Spirit's promptings to give above the tithe, *that* is honorable.

I believe the scriptural position regarding money is that we are to embrace biblical prosperity and renounce materialism at the same time. We can do both. We must do both. Poverty is always a blight. It demeans people. Even a cursory look at history and our world shows that wherever the gospel has taken root, there has always been an attending economic lift. Further, it will take massive economic strength for us to fulfill the Great Commission and bless all nations, as God commissions His followers to do.[6] At the same time we must renounce the spiritually deadening enticements of materialism. Life is not about stuff! It's about God, and it's about people. You cannot serve God and money.[7] You can have both, but you can't serve both. If we steward our finances well, we will also be free from its clutches.

Pastor Jerry Cook shared a beautiful illustration of a genuinely Christian heart of giving: "I've been to the highlands of New Guinea, where people live in abject poverty. One day my host took me into the countryside and said, 'Pick out the Christians' gardens.' I looked, and sure enough, the gardens of the believers were producing better than those of the nonbelievers. 'We pray over our gardens,' my host explained. 'We want to grow enough food to share with our neighbors who cannot pray God's blessings on their gardens as we do.'"[8] That kind of heart will not go unrewarded.

The side of town one lives on or the make of car one drives is really not the issue. As Pastor Cook reminds us, "What I'm doing with my resources says infinitely more about my spiritual condition than does the fact that I have them."[9]

"Before Jesus" in Use of Time

Thomas Carlyle wrote, "He who has no vision of eternity will never get a true grasp of time." One of the best barometers of our true spiritual condition is how we use our free time. One-third of our time is already spoken for in work. Another third we give to sleep. But that leaves approximately *eight hours each day* to invest as we choose. Whether we admit it or not, most of us end up doing pretty much what we want to do much of the time. But will our use of time stand the test at the judgment seat of Christ?

Leadership consultant Stephen Covey teaches that one of the most fruitful uses of time is to do what is "important but not urgent." This would include relationship building, planning, recreation, and recognizing and responding to new opportunities.[10] Time can be spent, or it can be invested. Clear priorities should mark our use of time.

First and foremost, we should give time to God. This sets the tone for any other expenditure of time. We will not be at our best, emotionally or otherwise, if we do not daily cultivate our relationship with God by spending time in His presence. R. T. Kendall reminds us, "When you stand before the Lord you may well regret how you used so much of your time, but I can safely promise that you will not regret a single minute you spent alone with God."[11]

Then we should give high priority to our families. No relationship can be nurtured without the investment of time. Yet frightening statistics have emerged concerning the sparse amount of actual time spent between parents and children. No doubt the same is true for time invested in developing our second most important relationship—with our spouses. Mentoring within families usually occurs in bits and pieces, but it cannot happen at all if parents are AWOL. Time is the soil into which we sow our love and concern. If little is sown, there will be little harvest.

We are also to invest time with our extended family, the church. And even beyond our local church, we are to give time and care to the entire body of Christ. The Bible teaches we are to do good to everyone, but especially to those who are of the household of faith.[12]

We must also reserve time to invest in God's purposes in our generation. True spirituality never happens in a vacuum. The end result of all our relationship development with God is to bring others into His kingdom as well. For some this will involve a change of career or relocation in a present career, becoming a sort of tentmaker missionary.

Volunteer work in community projects, vacation time used for short-term missions projects, visits to hospitals and nursing homes—these should also be prayerfully included on the Christian's agenda. And remember—it's all recorded. What you do purely as unto the Lord *now* will be openly rewarded *then*. The best time management technique I know is to live in light of eternity.

That All Should Honor the Son

The point of all of this is that we're accountable for how we live. In heaven—at the judgment seat of Christ—we will give an account of our stewardship. Someday we will recount "before Jesus" how we managed our relationships, our money, our gifts, and our time. Jesus said that God the Father will one day deliver all judgment to Him. "For the Father judges no one, but has committed all judgment to the Son, that all should honor the Son just as they honor the Father" (John 5:22–23).

"You have been commissioned to manage an asset for your Master," writes Bruce Wilkinson. "Your asset is your life—the sum of your talents, strengths, personality, and interests. Your opportunity is to manage your life in such a way that you greatly increase your Master's kingdom."[13]

You have a scheduled, personal appointment with Jesus. It will be your final exam. With our imperfect technology (which is no match for heaven's capabilities) we can access instant replays or download other past events on JumboTrons. What will our review at heaven's *bema* look like? It is not at all far-fetched to imagine that your personal audit before Jesus on that day could sound a lot like this:

- "I gave you some natural talents and spiritual gifts. Did you bear fruit? How much? Did you multiply your influence in My behalf? Did you develop those talents and gifts? Let's review how you used them for My kingdom's purposes."

- "Let's look at the records on how you apportioned your money. Did you pay your bills—on time? Did you invest in getting My name known worldwide? Did you advance My causes with your money? Did you remember the poor? And when you gave, what were your motives?"

- "How did your treat your wife? Did you love her as I love you? Did you learn to grow together toward the oneness of heart I had in mind as My gift to you both? Were you faithful to her—not just physically but mentally also? Did you cherish and love her with such faithfulness that her heart rested secure and you actually helped prepare her for her review with Me?"

- "What about your children? Did your words and your actions affirm them? Were you committed to transferring My truth to them—and to their friends? Did you bring them up in My training and instruction?"

- "All the people I sovereignly intersected with your life— how did you treat them? Did you minister My redemptive life to them?"

- "You lived in a wicked season on Earth. But you also had great information and opportunities literally at your fingertips. What books and magazines did you read? What level of priority did you give My written Word? Let's review how you used the Internet."

- "I gave you a set amount of years on Earth. Let's see what you thought was really important. Let's review where you put your money, whom you most enjoyed being with, and how you used your time. Let's check *why* you did what you did."

- "Were My concerns yours? Were My griefs yours? Were My joys your joys? Did you perceive what I was up to in the world during your lifetime? Were you courageous? Were you loving? Did you represent Me well as My ambassador? Did you nurture the fruit of My Spirit? How did your life advance My purposes?"

And then—He might ask the most chilling question of all: *Is that your final answer?*

Well...just a little of this sanctified musing stokes a healthy, reverential fear of the Lord. Thinking of this great final accounting, R. T. Kendall writes, "It seems to me that our hearts will be pounding out of our chests. Surely it will be the most sobering, terrifying moment we have ever experienced.... We will not be rewarded because of a gift God has given us. Joseph will not be rewarded in heaven because he received prophetic dreams or knew how to interpret dreams. The apostle Paul will not be rewarded in heaven because of his high IQ. It is *obedience* that will bring the reward."[14]

No wonder Paul wrote, "So we make it our goal to please him.... For we must all appear before the judgment seat of Christ, that each one may receive what is due him for the things done while in the body, whether good or bad. Since, then, we know what it is to fear the Lord, we try to persuade men" (2 Cor. 5:9–11, NIV).

How *will* we answer such personal probing by the Lord Jesus? As the song asks, "Will we be able to speak at all?" If we do, will we respond to the Lord with joy and confidence? Or will we try to sputter out a reason as to why we were spiritually semi-conscious during much of our earthly sojourn?

You cannot recover lost years—but God can! The Bible promises that, for those who not only regret but also repent over lost time, He will "restore…the years the swarming locust has eaten."[15] This miracle can be yours starting today as you crown Jesus Lord of the years that are left to you.

> When I stand at the judgment seat of Christ,
> And He shows His plan for me,
> The plan of my life as it might have been,
> Had He had His way, and I see
> How I blocked Him here, and checked Him there,
> And I would not yield my will,
> Will there be grief in my Savior's eyes,
> Grief though He loves me still?
> Would He have me rich and I stand there poor,
> Stripped of all but His grace,
> While memory runs like a hunted thing
> Down the paths I cannot retrace?
> Lord, of the years that are left to me,
> I give them to Thy hand;
> Take me and break me and mold me
> To the pattern Thou hast planned.
>
> —AUTHOR UNKNOWN

CHAPTER NINE

VINDICATED AT LAST!

Your Father who sees in secret will reward you openly.

—MATTHEW 6:4

Heaven still guards the right.[1]

—WILLIAM SHAKESPEARE

Y OU CANNOT WALK VERY FAR WITH JESUS BEFORE YOU ARE criticized and your motives are impugned.

Missionary author Amy Carmichael understood this. "Hast Thou No Scar," her classic poem regarding the cost of following Jesus, asks if it is even possible to truly serve Him without some battle scars.

Hast thou no scar?
No hidden scar on foot, or side, or hand?
I hear thee sung as mighty in the land,
I hear them hail thy bright ascendant star,
Hast thou no scar?

Hast thou no wound?
Yet I was wounded by the archers, spent,
Leaned Me against a tree to die; and rent
By ravening beasts that compassed Me, I swooned:
Hast thou no wound?

No wound? No scar?
Yet, as the Master shall the servant be,
and pierced are the feet that follow Me;
But thine are whole: can he have followed far
Who has no wound nor scar?[2]

Those dearest to us can sometimes inflict the deepest gashes. I heard a noted minister say, "I've been maligned, slandered, libeled, cursed—and that's just by my Christian brothers!"

Many Christians could identify with him. Out of the hurt of such rejection, it is natural to attempt defense and vindication. Yet any self-defense would only muddy the waters. Others may take the defense of the maligned person as an implication of his guilt. Yet we live in a time when striking back is the name of the game. "I don't get mad; I get even" seems to be the slogan even many Christians embrace.

But this vindictiveness, even when we're sorely wronged or misjudged, may say more about the victims than the assailants. This era of countersuits, getting even, and mutually assured destruction ("If you hurt me, I'll bury you"), even among Christians, is completely foreign to the spirit of Jesus. This jockeying for position and an "eye for an eye" mentality is, at best, an old covenant allowance and, at worst, unholy fire fueled by demons.

When Jesus was falsely accused, He did not open His mouth in rebuttal. Graphically, the Bible says He was led as a lamb to the slaughter.[3] Peter wrote, "Christ suffered for you, leaving you an example, that you should follow in his steps. 'He committed no sin, and no deceit was found in his mouth.' When they hurled their insults at him, he did not retaliate; when he suffered, he made no threats. Instead, he entrusted himself to him who judges justly" (1 Pet. 2:21–23, NIV).

It is this decision to entrust ourselves to God for His ultimate vindication that enables us to endure the blasts against us in the present. Our model for endurance is Jesus. Amidst the most vicious verbal and physical abuse, He endured patiently. What gave Him such strength? He saw another world and final vindication by His Father.

Do you "see" with spiritual eyes that world to come and heaven's holy hosts that even now are watching how you live out your days here? Today, and every day, you have an unseen audience:

> Therefore we also, since we are surrounded by so great a cloud of witnesses, let us lay aside every weight, and the sin which so easily ensnares us, and let us run with endurance the race that is set before us, looking unto Jesus, the author and finisher of our faith, who for the joy that was set before Him endured the cross, despising the shame, and has sat down at the right hand of the throne of God. For consider Him who endured such hostility from sinners against Himself, lest you become weary and discouraged in your souls.
>
> —HEBREWS 12:1–3

When you are assaulted for living in heaven's honor, it's easy to want to throw in the towel. After all, such attacks are unfair, unwarranted. Some people even make it a game to accost Christians in every way possible, hoping they can get believers to compromise. If a Christian compromises his convictions, then his life is no longer a rebuke to those who do not acknowledge Christ's lordship.

Almost all serious followers of Jesus today worldwide are challenged at some level. Some are merely harassed. At present, this harassment is what believers in the United States and much of Europe experience. Others face stiffer opposition; they are persecuted. And some Christians—about 120,000 every year—pay the ultimate price for their allegiance to Christ; they are martyred. They are those "of whom the world was not worthy" (Heb. 11:38). This ultimate gift to Jesus remains, in Ed Silvoso's words, "a possibility on standby" for every follower of Christ.

We are assured that "*all* who desire to live godly in Christ Jesus will suffer persecution" (2 Tim. 3:12, emphasis added). So we need to link arms in solidarity with our brothers and sisters worldwide. The American church in particular is far too myopic and self-indulged. We are called to align ourselves with the persecuted church. "Remember those in prison as if you were their fellow prisoners, and those who are mistreated as if you yourselves were suffering" (Heb. 13:3, NIV).

So when you're tempted to compromise because of attacks against you, remember that others in your family suffer, too. Look to Jesus. At those times of discouragement and emotional injury, look to Jesus. And look ahead to your coming reward. When people attack you because of your faith, great is your reward in heaven: "Blessed are those who are persecuted for righteousness' sake, for theirs is the kingdom of heaven. Blessed are you when they revile and persecute you, and say all kinds of evil against you falsely for My sake. Rejoice and be exceedingly glad, for great is your reward in heaven" (Matt. 5:10–12). Endurance to keep running, not turning your attention to distractions, comes from trusting God to vindicate you in the end. Moses aligned with God's people and took the heat for it, specifically because he "[esteemed] the reproach of Christ greater riches than the treasures in Egypt; for he looked to the reward" (Heb. 11:26). Moses looked past the present, material treasures of Egypt to the real, enduring treasures of heaven. The King James Version says, "He had respect unto the recompense of the reward." May we respect heaven's rewards, too. May we live in heaven's honor.

Life's Few "Musts"

Over the triple doorways of the magnificent Cathedral of Milan there are three inscriptions spanning the ornate arches. In one arch is carved a wreath of roses and the legend, "All that which pleases is but for a moment." In the other is carved a cross and the words, "All that which troubles is but for a moment." But in the arch over the great central entrance to the main aisle is the inscription, "That only is important which is eternal."

What a sermon! Our pleasures are momentary. So are our trials. What matters is what is eternal. Accusations will come and go. Time heals many wounds. Circumstances change constantly. But we are moving toward an eternal world and an eternal God. Our paramount desire, then, should be to spend our energies on eternal pursuits.

There are only a few things in life that absolutely have to occur. Those few "musts," however, are extremely important. Here are three.

First, if you are going to heaven at all, you *must* be born again. You must experience the inner, spiritual rebirth through faith in Christ that qualifies you for citizenship in heaven.[4]

The gospel invitation is to "whosoever will" (Rev. 22:17, KJV). No one comes to Christ against his or her will. The offer of salvation is completely optional. But once you come to Christ the picture changes. You're in the army now—the Lord's army, and here is the second "must." The draft is voluntary, but once inducted, you *must* obey the orders of the Captain. For instance, Christ's Great Commission is not the Great Suggestion. It's a mandate for all believers. We are given the mission to turn His foes into His friends.

The third imperative, after your heavenly credentials are established, is an appointment scheduled for you that is not optional. You *must* stand before the judgment seat of Christ.[5] The word *judgment* in this term "the judgment seat of Christ," is the Greek word *bema* or *bematos*. It refers to a raised platform on which a judge stood to render arbitrations or rewards. This term is used ten times in the New Testament. It was a place of inspection, a place where performances were judged. Every athlete in the ancient Olympic games was familiar with the *bema*. It would be similar to that place at our modern games where the winners receive their medals from the judges.

The judgment seat of Christ is *not* to determine whether we will go to heaven. That is determined at the Great White Throne Judgment, and the criterion is clear. Only those whose names are written in the Lamb's Book of Life are granted access into heaven.[6] And your name is placed in that book only by renouncing sin and placing your faith in Jesus Christ as Savior and Lord.

But at the judgment seat your entire postconversion life will come up for review. This will be the time when rewards for all qualifying Christians are meted out. This is where our position, if any, of ruling with Christ in His eternal kingdom will be determined. "The judgment seat of Christ," writes Rick Howard, "is the posting of the exam grades, the evaluation of our life's choices, and the establishment of our position for eternity."[7] In light of this coming event in which your heart's secrets will be exposed and from which there is no escape, it is vital to always keep this upcoming "must" in view. This enables you to live today for what matters forever.

When we really want a friend to join us at some event, we may put on some pressure and tell him, "You just *have to* be there." Well, trust me, there's no opting out of this big event. You just have to be there. And so do I. So we had better get ready.

HOLY—IN THE TWENTY-FIRST CENTURY

Since you will stand soon before a perfectly holy God, you should prepare your heart in holiness. But the very word *holiness* has fallen on hard times these days. Even some Christians mock the popular concept of "holiness," complete with its hypocrisy and holier-than-thou-ism.

But this is a distorted perception. C. S. Lewis wrote, "How little people know who think that holiness is dull. When one meets the real thing...it is irresistible. If even 10 percent of the world's population had it, would not the whole world be happy and converted before a year's end?"[8]

True holiness is light-years removed from self-righteousness. Self-righteousness is just that—a supposed goodness that is induced by one's own self. The biblical understanding of both righteousness and holiness is that they are produced and sustained by God alone, but with our cooperation. This is one of the unique features of the Christian faith. All other major religions are primarily an attempt on man's part to induce proper living and thus be accepted by some deity. But "in the gospel a righteousness from God is revealed, a righteousness that is by faith from first to last, just as it is written: 'The righteous will live by faith'" (Rom. 1:17, NIV).

The very life of God is implanted in us by the new birth Jesus spoke of. This life is nurtured by obedience to the promptings of God's indwelling Spirit. Increased obedience produces increased sensitivity to sin. And this is the great need of our day. Our generation has become drugged and desensitized to sin and its effects.

What then is the antidote? A megadose of genuine holiness. And this is not merely for the mystics or the self-styled spiritual. It is for all who belong to Christ. There is a segment of the church that is referred to as "the holiness movement." Actually, the entire church should be the holiness movement! God's Word is absolutely clear: "As He who called you is holy, you also be holy in all your conduct" (1 Pet. 1:15).

Biblical holiness does not seem to be a primary concern to American Christians. There's a reason: "Worldly Christianity is simply heavenless Christianity," writes Ted Dekker. "In so many teachings and books designed to prod us into successful Christian living, there's a preoccupation with life on earth. In many ways we have become our own greatest enemy."[9]

George Barna laments, "The Bible clearly states that true believers should be readily distinguished from nonbelievers by the way they live. Yet, the evidence undeniably suggests that most American Christians today do not live in a way that is quantifiably different from their non-Christian peers, in spite of the fact that they profess to believe in a set of principles that should set them apart."[10]

I was appalled to hear the story of a professing Christian teenager, a young man I know. His girlfriend had found out that she was pregnant. (This in itself shows that holiness was not a high priority.) This young couple determined to take what seemed the easiest course; she would have an abortion. As they were driving to the abortion clinic, the young man saw a stray dog with a broken leg. Immediately he stopped his car and, with a heart full of compassion for the lame animal, he took the dog to the veterinarian, paying all expenses. Then he personally nursed the dog back to health.

Dear God, what has happened to us? This young man's conscience was highly sensitized to the plight of a stray dog, but he was about to murder his own baby! It is past time for a moral revolution. John Wesley's plea to his hearers needs to echo in our ears today: "O that you may now give yourselves to Him who gave Himself for you, in humble faith, and in holy, active, patient love! So shall you rejoice with exceeding joy in His day, when He shall come in the clouds of heaven."[11]

THE IMPARTIAL JUDGE

Someone has suggested that these days Lady Justice is blindfolded, not because she is impartial but because she is embarrassed by the bizarre verdicts of some judges. With a judicial system increasingly skewed by money under the table, backroom deals, and legislating from the bench, it would be hard for me to even retain the concept of pure justice—were it not for my confidence that there is a day coming when a perfectly impartial Judge will balance the scales.

Frankly, I don't think many Christians today have a clue that they are headed for an appearance before the Judge of the universe to give an account of their every action, word, thought, and motive. James reminds us that "the Judge stands at the door."[12] In his classic work *Imitation of Christ,* Thomas à Kempis warned, "At every turn of your life, keep the end in view; remembering that you will have to stand before a strict Judge.... Strange, that you should look forward so little to the Day of Judgment, when there will be no counsel to plead for you..."

Such tough words are difficult for Christians today (including me) to read. Yet we need to read them, and we need to be reminded of just how sobering the judgment seat of Christ is. In fact, Paul was speaking of our appearance before the judgment seat when he used one of his most pungent, even frightening phrases—"the terror of the Lord" (2 Cor. 5:11). The Greek word used in this case for "terror" is *phobos,* a strong word from which we get our word *phobia*. There's no way to spin this and be true to the text. Standing before our perfectly holy Lord and God will be—let me search for a little milder word—unnerving, to say the least. But to fear the Lord—and this is important—does not mean we are to be frightened of Him. Rather, Bible scholar W. E. Vine described this fear of God as "a controlling motive of the life, in matters spiritual and moral, not a mere fear of His power and righteous retribution, but a wholesome dread of displeasing Him, a fear which banishes the terror that shrinks from His presence."[13] "For you did not receive the spirit of bondage again to fear, but you received the Spirit of adoption by whom we cry out, 'Abba, Father'" (Rom. 8:15).

Remember back to your school days when your teacher would suddenly announce, without warning, a "pop test." A quick streak of terror might have raced down your spine. Now, what if the teacher announced that this wasn't a pop test, but that it was your final exam? The fear factor would shoot up. One day we will suddenly be called to account. Questions will be taken "from the whole book"—from all of your life since you have known Jesus Christ. The only confidence you and I will have on that day is to stay perpetually prepared.

I think it's important to include a balancing word here. Jesus is not only our judge. He is also—this very day—our love-filled advocate. He is on the job right now as our divine defense attorney, pleading our case before the Father. "He lives forever to plead with God on [our] behalf" (Heb. 7:25, NLT). So, it's encouraging to remember that the impartial, perfectly holy judge you will face also loves you so deeply that He died for you. And every day since you came to Him in faith He has been in your corner, defending you.

Still, accurate records are being kept of each life. And we will recall before our Judge every detail of our lives, including our careless words. But the Bible teaches that our righteous deeds will also follow us into heaven. Positions of authority in the world to come along with the rewards and treasures we receive in heaven will forever remind us of godly choices we made here on Earth.[16] Malachi 3:16 (NIV) says a "scroll of remembrance" is maintained of those who fear the Lord and meditate on His name.

We don't know when death or Christ's coming will call us to account. But we do know it will happen. We can prepare now by sensitizing our hearts. There really is no middle ground. And the time to face it is now.

Paul determined to judge neither others nor himself prematurely. "Therefore judge nothing before the appointed time," he wrote. "Wait till the Lord comes. He will bring to light what is hidden in darkness and will expose the motives of men's hearts" (1 Cor. 4:5, NIV). For the person who thinks concerning his sin, "I got away with it"—you didn't. "Some men's sins are clearly evident, preceding them to judgment, but those of some men follow later" (1 Tim. 5:24). The inverse is also true. If you thought your good deeds were performed only for an audience of One—they weren't. One day they too will be brought to light and publicly rewarded: "Likewise, the good works of some are clearly evident, and those that are otherwise cannot be hidden" (1 Tim. 5:25).

We can safely entrust to Him all our hopes, all our weaknesses, and all our confidence that He will grant us not only a home in heaven but also treasures there. "For I know whom I have believed and am persuaded that He is able to keep what I have committed to Him until that Day" (2 Tim. 1:12).

The understanding that we will stand before the Lord is certainly an impetus to holiness. But it is also a prod to steadiness and patience. For on that day, the scales will be forever balanced. Then the false accusations against you will be seen for what they were. Then your true motives will be revealed. This is not just a warning; it's also an encouragement.

Hebrews 11:35–37 tells of a magnificent group of heaven-focused believers who "were tortured, not accepting deliverance, that they might obtain a better resurrection. Still others had trial of mockings and scourgings, yes, and of chains and imprisonment. They were stoned, they were sawn in two, were tempted, were slain with the sword." They were willing to forgo an easier path now for eternal accolades then. Multitudes who have suffered in silence will be honored publicly. Those followers of Jesus who have chosen, like their Lord, to stay silent while their lives and characters were unjustly maligned will be vindicated at last.

CHAPTER TEN

A Sure Reward

By faith Moses, when he had grown up, refused to be known as the son of Pharaoh's daughter. He chose to be mistreated along with the people of God rather than to enjoy the pleasures of sin for a short time. He regarded disgrace for the sake of Christ as of greater value than the treasures of Egypt, because he was looking ahead to his reward.

—Hebrews 11:24–26, niv

That which seems so real, so imminent, so sure will ultimately give place to what can never pass away and which is of greatest value and ultimate significance.[1]

—Stuart McAllister

ALBERT EINSTEIN WAS ONE OF THE GREAT GENIUSES OF THE twentieth century. Among many accomplishments, his work helped produce the data necessary for splitting the atom. He also realized the potential for destruction that such a discovery held. One starlit night Professor Einstein was walking across the Princeton Promenade with some of his students. He stopped for a moment and gazed into the starry heavens. He sighed and said, "Anyway, *that* the atom cannot destroy."

There are some things that will abide, come what may. The universe is permanent. It is the dwelling of the eternal God: "Thus says the LORD: 'Heaven is My throne, and earth is My footstool'" (Isa. 66:1). The Word of God also transcends time: "Forever, O LORD, Your word is settled in heaven" (Ps. 119:89). And the blessings with which heaven will one day reward the faithful are also permanent: "He who sows righteousness (moral and spiritual rectitude in every area and relation) shall have a sure reward [permanent and satisfying]" (Prov. 11:18, AMP).

The wise course of action, then, is to pursue the permanent, to seek that which is so strong and lasting that corrosion cannot devalue it and thieves cannot displace it. This life's treasures often die a sudden, premature death. Acclaim is fleeting. Riches, as we've already seen, can take wings and fly away. Virility and charm can vanish at the merciless hands of disease. No matter how much we may nip, tuck, or staple, age eventually trumps youth. Only the treasures of the afterlife live on.

GOOD AND FAITHFUL

In the parable of the talents, the master commends the faithful servant with these words: "Well done, good and faithful servant; you were faithful over a few things, I will make you ruler over many things. Enter into the joy of your lord" (Matt. 25:21). In this statement, two strong motives emerge. The first is affirmation. There is immense power in desiring accolades from someone we love or esteem. To hear Jesus say, "Well done"—what a driving motivation! Then there is the motive of increased influence: "I will make you ruler over many things." Hope of eternal gain in heaven for faithful, fruitful service for Christ on Earth is not only scriptural, but it is also meant to act as a potent stimulus to live in heaven's honor.

Not only do two motives emerge from this passage; two qualifications surface as well. The first is simple goodness. The servant who receives accolades from his master is a good servant. No doubt this means that he is good at what he does; he is a good servant. But surely it also implies that the servant himself is good. This carries the idea of a pure heart, not motivated by a usurping lust for power. With the psalmist the good servant can say, "LORD, my heart is not haughty, nor my eyes lofty. Neither do I concern myself with great matters, nor with things too profound for me" (Ps. 131:1). In other words, he knows his niche and functions effectively in it.

The good servant is also faithful. He is not looking for promotion from some outside source. He has a personal commitment to his master and fully intends to serve him the rest of his life. He is faithful to his task and faithful to his master, year in and year out. He doesn't chronically call in sick. He doesn't scheme ways to get out of work. He's just there, on the job, for his master.

Such workers are in short supply today. Companies lose millions of dollars because of employee laziness and disloyalty. We talk much today about the need for assertive leadership. But if there is a crying need for leaders, there is a bellowing need for good and faithful servants.

What produces these qualities in servants? Foremost, it is love for the master. The servant seeks to please his master because he loves him. Just so, something in the deepest part of every true Christian longs to be pleasing to Jesus: "We love Him because He first loved us" (1 John 4:19). Consequently, when a Christian sins, he not only grieves the Holy Spirit, but he also grieves himself. Yes, it is possible for a Christian to sin. But it is impossible for him to sin without remorse. Love for our Master, though His ways may sometimes seem strange and difficult, produces the side effects of goodness and faithfulness.

This becomes especially important when we call believers to sacrificial service. As one veteran missionary said, "The need can get you there, but only the love of Christ can keep you there." If we recruit with any motivation other than Christ's love, those who go out in a tide of emotion will get backwashed in a sea of disillusionment.

The love of Christ is a higher, nobler motivation for service than the potential of rewards. But this does not mean that we are to dismiss rewards as a legitimate stimulus to faithfulness. The Bible is replete with the principle of rewards. Hebrews 11:6 refers to God as a rewarder. It's part of His character. When we remember that God is a rewarder, it will make a practical, verifiable difference in the way we live our lives. We should value heaven's rewards because Jesus deems them valuable. And you can be sure Jesus would not offer you anything that was not infinitely beyond price.

AN AWESOME BUSINESS

The Bible speaks of several different types of rewards in the afterlife. Usually, there are very clear guidelines prescribed for attaining these rewards. It needs to be noted again that salvation itself is *not* a reward; it is a gift of God's grace. It is given freely to all who turn from their sins and commit their lives to Christ: "Not by works of righteousness which we have done, but according to His mercy He saved us, through the washing of regeneration and renewing of the Holy Spirit" (Titus 3:5). Heaven is a free gift, but rewards are just that—rewards. They are given for meeting specific biblical qualifications. To qualify for salvation one only needs to be a sinner in need of forgiveness. When we come to Christ in repentance and faith, we are saved. But there are clear biblical criteria for heaven's rewards, and they all have to do with obedience.

First, you will be rewarded for pursuing your relationship with God through spiritual disciplines like prayer and fasting. "When you pray, go into your room, and when you have shut your door, pray to your Father who is in the secret place; and your Father who sees in secret will reward you openly" (Matt. 6:6). Godliness always brings rewards, both now and later: "Godliness is profitable for all things, having promise of the life that now is and of that which is to come" (1 Tim. 4:8). John Bevere says it well: "We are to run in this life to win. In order to win, we must develop discipline and self-control and live with purpose. We are not competing against others, only ourselves, and our goal is to be well-pleasing to Jesus in everything we do."[2]

Then Scripture speaks of rewards for good deeds and costly service to the Lord. For instance, winning people to Christ and pointing them toward a God-honoring life brings immediate blessings. But it also produces vast benefits in heaven: "Those who are wise shall shine like the brightness of the firmament, and those who turn many to righteousness like the stars forever and ever" (Dan. 12:3). Other acts of self-denial will also be rewarded:

> If anyone desires to come after Me, let him deny himself, and take up his cross, and follow Me. For whoever desires to save his life will lose it, but whoever loses his life for My sake will find it. For what profit is it to a man if he gains the whole world, and loses his own soul? Or what will a man give in exchange for his soul? For the Son of Man will come in the glory of His Father with His angels, and then He will reward each according to his works.
>
> —MATTHEW 16:24–27

Also, helping the poor out of one's own need has a heavenly payoff: "Sell what you have and give to those in need. This will store up treasure for you in heaven!" (Luke 12:33, NLT).

Then there is the promise that those who faithfully serve masters (or in our case, employers) will be rewarded.[3] Christians are told to work at all times "not with eyeservice, as men-pleasers, but as bondservants of Christ, doing the will of God from the heart, with good will doing service, as to the Lord, and not to men, knowing that whatever good anyone does, he will receive the same from the Lord" (Eph. 6:6–8).

Not to be forgotten is the ministry of hospitality, especially as it affects receiving ministers (prophets) and other godly people.[4] The hospitable believer will share in their reward. Jesus said, "He who receives a prophet in the name of a prophet shall receive a prophet's reward. And he who receives a righteous man in the name of a righteous man shall receive a righteous man's reward" (Matt. 10:41).

Then the Bible says there are rewards in the afterlife for sufferings in this one. Peter reminds us, "Beloved, do not think it strange concerning the fiery trial which is to try you, as though some strange thing happened to you; but rejoice to the extent that you partake of Christ's sufferings, that when His glory is revealed, you may also be glad with exceeding joy" (1 Pet. 4:12–13). Although some are teaching that trials for a Christian are a "strange thing," the Bible says to expect them and profit from them. When persecutions come because we take a stand for righteousness, Jesus said to "rejoice and be exceedingly glad, for great is your reward in heaven" (Matt. 5:12).

Scripture also teaches that we will be rewarded in kind for a life of mercy and kindness. Mercy sown by you will reap mercy extended to you: "Blessed are the merciful, for they shall obtain mercy" (Matt. 5:7).

John Bevere reminds us, "Not only will our works be examined, but our thoughts, motives, and intentions as well. This is why it is so crucial for believers to carefully listen to, heed, and hide in our hearts the Word of God, for it is continually 'exposing and sifting and analyzing and judging the very thoughts and purposes of the heart' (Heb. 4:12, AMP). Nothing else can get to the depths of our heart as His Word."5

When I was a boy in Sunday school, we used to sing a song that advised us to be careful about what we saw, said, and did. Why? "For the Father up above is looking down in love / so be careful, little hands, what you do." Theologian J. I. Packer gives us the same encouragement to remember that God is always watching: "Living becomes an awesome business," he writes, "when you realize that you spend every moment of your life in the sight and company of an omniscient, omnipresent Creator."6

Purity of life produces a vessel of honor, set apart for God's purposes. "Therefore, if anyone cleanses himself from what is dishonorable, he will be a vessel for honorable use, set apart as holy, useful to the master of the house; ready for every good work" (2 Tim. 2:21, ESV). Humility and a servant's heart will qualify you for greatness in the kingdom of heaven: "Therefore whoever humbles himself as this little child is the greatest in the kingdom of heaven" (Matt. 18:4).

Increased authority is awarded for faithfulness in your present assignment: "You were faithful over a few things, I will make you ruler over many things" (Matt. 25:21).

From these passages and the entire tone of the Bible, it's clear that God rewards those who pursue His favor. "He is a rewarder of those who diligently seek Him" (Heb. 11:6). To be indifferent to His offer of rewards is to despise His character. God is a giver.

PAY THE COST

Since God has given us His best in Jesus Christ, it naturally follows that we should give Him our best. Yet too often only the leftovers are given to Him. One of the tragedies of much of contemporary Christianity is that our best hours, finest efforts, the majority of our money, our influence— these are often expended on selfish pursuits. Whatever is left, if anything, is then piously offered to God with the inference that He ought to be really happy He's getting anything.

Such an attitude, if not blasphemous, is certainly unworthy of the majestic God who rules heaven and Earth. After David's disobedience to God's command, the king prepared to bring a sin offering to God. David had sinned against the Lord by numbering the people—looking at bigness and trusting in the size of the nation and his army. God had judged David's disobedience by sending a plague that wiped out seventy thousand people. David, now fully repentant, had found a suitable place to build an altar—on the threshing floor owned by Araunah. King David's subject Araunah graciously offered to give the property to his king at no cost. David's classic answer mirrors a heart of costly commitment: "No, but I will surely buy it from you for a price; nor will I offer burnt offerings to the LORD my God with that which costs me nothing" (2 Sam. 24:24).

How would you rate the quality of what you offer to God? Does what you bring to God cost you something?

There is no such thing in athletics as training for glory without experiencing a personal cost. You learn to suffer for a future reward. You know that glory has its cost, and there are no discounts. The late Tom Landry, longtime coach of the Dallas Cowboys and an ardent Christian, said, "My job is to get men to do what they don't want to do in order to achieve what they've always wanted to achieve." Do you want eternal rewards in heaven? There's a cost, and there are no discounts. As Dwight Eisenhower observed, "There are no victories at bargain basement prices."

Yet, amazingly, many Christians seem to think they will be "carried to the skies on flowery beds of ease." This phrase comes from Isaac Watts's majestic hymn "Am I a Soldier of the Cross?" This particular verse challenges present-day believers to identify with those who have endured spiritual attacks in order to advance the gospel.

> Must I be carried to the skies
> On flowery beds of ease,
> While others fought to win the prize,
> And sailed through bloody seas?

Watts then answered this rhetorical question with the reminder that those who will one day reign with Christ must also endure opposition for the fame of His name. "If we endure hardship, we will reign with him" (2 Tim. 2:12, NLT).

> Sure I must fight if I would reign;
> Increase my courage, Lord!
> I'll bear the toil, endure the pain,
> Supported by Thy Word.[7]

We must understand that anything that's worth anything costs something. In a statement almost completely alien to Western Christianity, the Scriptures say that Moses *chose to suffer affliction* with the people of God rather than enjoy the temporal pleasures of sin. Why did he do it? What would make anyone forgo immediate gratification and choose to suffer?

The answer is twofold. First, Moses realized that sin's pleasures have a very short shelf life. The gratification would have been only for a short time. The "stolen fruit" that is sweet to the taste sours almost immediately in the stomach. Second, Moses was allowed to see into the era of the new covenant, and he "[esteemed] the reproach of Christ greater riches than the treasures in Egypt; for he looked to the reward" (Heb. 11:26). Moses was strengthened to resist the easy way out by looking to a coming reward.

Throughout church history many unsung heroes have been "tortured, not accepting deliverance, that they might obtain a better resurrection" (Heb. 11:35). We speak often of faith for deliverance. But what immaculate faith is this that forgoes present deliverance in lieu of a more honored position in eternity!

Then there is Jesus Himself, "who for the joy that was set before Him endured the cross, despising the shame, and has sat down at the right hand of the throne of God" (Heb. 12:2). Jesus saw beyond the pain of the cross to His future glory and the joy of "bringing many sons to glory" (Heb. 2:10).

These all gave costly sacrifices to God. Why? They all saw with keener than normal perception a "joy that was set before them." Can you see it, too? Living in heaven's honor buoys us against sinking in despair. There's a bright tomorrow for those who give that which costs.

With all your being, you will want something tangible in your hands that heaven says is valuable to lay in worship at the feet of Jesus—not in payment for salvation, but in awestruck gratitude for it. So, count the cost. Then forget the cost. Just pay the cost.

UNIVERSAL LAWS

The hope of lasting rewards is predicated on two "givens," two immutable principles that have been woven by God into the very fabric of life. The first is that *those who humble themselves before God will be exalted by Him.* Because of its very nature we may not be able to detect whether or not we possess true humility, but a continual humbling of the soul before God is certainly a step in that direction. It is arrogance and self-sufficiency that bait us for the devil's trap.

It is battle enough to be opposed by Satan. But it is a far greater concern to be opposed by God Almighty because of pride. That battle cannot and should not be won. Instead we are to "be submissive to one another, and be clothed with humility, for 'God resists the proud, but gives grace to the humble.' Therefore humble yourselves under the mighty hand of God, that He may exalt you in due time" (1 Pet. 5:5–6). Andrew Murray said, "Our chief care, highest virtue, only happiness, now and through all eternity, is to present ourselves as empty vessels in which God can dwell and manifest His power and goodness."[8] Humble yourself in the sight of the Lord, and He will exalt you. Jesus promised that the meek will inherit the earth. This is far more than a religious platitude. It's a fact. In Christ's coming kingdom there will be a massive power reversal, and His humble servants will then rule and reign with Him.

This brings us to the second universal law. *We will reap exactly what we sow.* God's Word urges us, "Sow for yourselves righteousness; reap in mercy; break up your fallow ground, for it is time to seek the Lord, till He comes and rains righteousness on you" (Hosea 10:12).

Many today seem to be sowing to the flesh and praying for a crop failure. Yet Scripture is clear: "Do not be deceived, God is not mocked; for whatever a man sows, that he will also reap. For he who sows to his flesh will of the flesh reap corruption, but he who sows to the Spirit will of the Spirit reap everlasting life. And let us not grow weary while doing good, for in due season we shall reap if we do not lose heart" (Gal. 6:7–9).

To some extent, the "due season" is in this life. There are plenty of blessings to harvest for right living down here. But the full crop of righteousness sown is reaped in the afterlife. Keep sowing. Your "due season" will come. And like other faithful servants, you will enter into the joy of your Lord.

CHAPTER ELEVEN

TREASURES IN HEAVEN

Do not lay up for yourselves treasures on earth, where moth and rust destroy and where thieves break in and steal; but lay up for yourselves treasures in heaven, where neither moth nor rust destroys and where thieves do not break in and steal. For where your treasure is, there your heart will be also.

—MATTHEW 6:19–21

What would happen to the church if Christians came to believe that the rewards God wants to give us exceed the value of an Olympic gold medal by a millionfold? That is not an overexaggeration; it is an underexaggeration.

—RICK HOWARD

IN AN ANCIENT GREEK FABLE, THE SWIFT-FOOTED ATALANTA, confident of her success, challenged everyone to race her. Finally, Hippomenes accepted her challenge, and the race began.

As expected, Atalanta took an early and commanding lead. But then Hippomenes did something completely unexpected. Taking a beautiful apple from his pocket, he tossed it alongside Atalanta's path as she ran. Immediately Atalanta was distracted as the apple shimmered in the sun, and Hippomenes overtook her. Soon Atalanta remembered the race and, dropping the apple, retook the lead.

But wait. Once again Hippomenes dropped a golden apple at Atalanta's feet. Once again she temporarily lost her focus and her lead, only to recover it again.

Then they were stretching toward the finish. The end of the race was in sight. A third and final time Hippomenes tossed out a beautiful apple. This time Atalanta's roving eye was her undoing. Sidetracked by its beauty, she paused. And this time, because of their closeness to the finish line, she never retook the lead. Hippomenes, by his craftiness, won the race.

This is an apt description of how the devil, your cunning adversary, pitches charming distractions along your path to slow and even stop you. A fundamental rule of running a race is to never look back and never look around. Always keep your eyes on the goal. The attractive, deceptive fruit of the lust of the flesh, the lust of the eyes, and the pride of life will seek to allure you from focusing on the race.[1] But if your eyes are fixed on Jesus, their charm dims in comparison to Him.

> Let us throw off everything that hinders and the sin that so easily entangles, and let us run with perseverance the race marked out for us. Let us fix our eyes on Jesus, the author and perfecter of our faith.
> —HEBREWS 12:1–2, NIV

Stay focused on the finish line!

THAT DAY

Martin Luther remarked that there were only two days of importance on his calendar: today and "that day"—the day of the Lord. Luther understood that all the days of his earthly life were preparation for that awesome time when he would stand before Jesus and give an account for his life. Today is the only time we have to prepare for that day. And it is that day that gives full meaning to today.

One of Karl Marx's strong objections to Christianity as he perceived it was that Christians seemed to scare people into servility by warning of a coming day of judgment. Marx also believed the hope of heaven and of eternal rewards was a nonsensical dream concocted to relieve people of the pain of their present lives. To use his words, "Religion...is the opium of the people."[2]

To be sure, this coming big event can be caricatured and misrepresented. Yet that day—the day of Christ's dominion and the vindication of His loyal followers—is threaded throughout Scripture. The Bible teaches that it will come swiftly, as a thief in the night (2 Pet. 3:10). Scripture indicates that this "great and notable day of the Lord" will coincide with a worldwide outpouring of God's Spirit, unusual phenomena in the heavens, and the return of Jesus Christ to this planet.[3]

Scripture refers to this cataclysmic day with several terms—the great day, the day of the Lord, the day of Christ, and the day of God. Theologians sometimes refer to this unrivaled rule of the Messiah as "the consummation of all things in Christ." In each reference the point is clear: While *this day* belongs to man, *that day* belongs to Christ. He will have the last word on the destiny of this planet and its people.

It's interesting to me that many non-Christians choose Resurrection Sunday as their annual time to give God a tip of the hat. On Easter morning they forgo their usual Sunday routine to go to church and sing about a risen Redeemer. Yet it is this very fact of Christ's resurrection that ensures a coming judgment on a day already appointed by God—*that day*. God "now commands all men everywhere to repent, because He has appointed a day in which He will judge the world in righteousness by the Man whom He has ordained. He has given assurance of this to all by raising Him from the dead" (Acts 17:30–31). With every hymn that celebrates resurrection and with each reciting of the creed affirming belief that Jesus broke out of that tomb, the nonbeliever is reaffirming that the Judge is alive and that judgment is coming. The guarantee of impending judgment is Christ's resurrection—"He will judge the world in righteousness...He has given assurance of this by raising Him from the dead."

Whatever you may believe about the millennium, there are certain facts concerning that day that all Bible believers embrace. First, Scripture declares that day will be a day of *revelation*. Secrets tucked away securely in hearts will be disclosed. For the person living for Jesus this is not a threat but a hope. Each "cup of cold water" served without fanfare as unto the Lord will be openly rewarded on that day.[4] The faithful believer looks to this time when his true motives will be exposed.

In light of this coming disclosure, the believer should forgo judgment on even his own motives as well as the motives of others. While we should always welcome the Holy Spirit to examine our hearts, at the same time we should guard against an unhealthy, constant introspection. A young boy with a small carrot patch complained to his mother that his carrots weren't growing. "What's the matter?" his mother inquired. "Are you keeping the weeds pulled and giving your carrots enough water?"

"Oh, yes, Mother," the boy replied. "Not only that, but I also pull up my carrots every day to see if they're growing."

Often we pull up our sprouting growth with well-intentioned introspection. Hey, it's not about *us*; it's about *Him*. We should just let growth happen, nourished by the vine life of Jesus and the irrigating refreshing of His Spirit.

The apostle Paul acknowledged criticism of his ministry but deemed it "a very small thing" (1 Cor. 4:3). Further, he refrained from self-judgment. All such determinations are subjective and therefore faulty. We will either grade ourselves too high or too low. Also, our judgments are premature. Paul was content to forgo judgment on his life, by himself or by others. Rather, he would wait for the Lord's final assessment.

This willingness to wait for Christ's final verdict also helped keep Paul from being judgmental:

> But why do you judge your brother? Or why do you show contempt for your brother? For we shall all stand before the judgment seat of Christ. For it is written: "As I live, says the LORD, every knee shall bow to Me, and every tongue shall confess to God." So then each of

us shall give an account of himself to God. Therefore let us not judge one another anymore, but rather resolve this, not to put a stumbling block or a cause to fall in our brother's way.

—ROMANS 14:10–13

Second, that day is a day of *retribution.* The scales will be forever balanced. The inequities will be forever resolved. Paul was physically whipped by Pharisees and verbally whipped by some fellow Christians. Even some churches he helped to plant later questioned the validity of his ministry. After facing tribunals with predetermined bias against him, Paul looked forward to facing a righteous Judge whose only vested interest is in those He has redeemed. The apostle anticipated a reward for his faithfulness, "which the Lord, the righteous Judge, will give to me on that Day" (2 Tim. 4:8). Referring to Himself, Jesus said that "the Son of Man will come in the glory of His Father with His angels, and then He will reward each according to his works" (Matt. 16:27).

Third, that day will be a day of *reigning* for Jesus Christ. John says he was "in the Spirit on the Lord's Day" (Rev. 1:10). Many Bible scholars believe this is not a reference to a certain day of the week but to the coming day when Jesus reigns supreme over all creation. It was during this vision, on the Lord's Day, that Jesus Christ was revealed to John in almost indescribable splendor. Although this is Spirit-inspired Scripture, one senses that John is groping for words in our limited human vocabulary to describe the reigning King. "His head and His hair were white like wool, as white as snow, and His eyes like a flame of fire; His feet were like fine brass, as if refined in a furnace, and His voice as the sound of many waters; He had in His right hand seven stars, out of His mouth went a sharp two-edged sword, and His countenance was like the sun shining in its strength. And when I saw Him, I fell at His feet as dead" (Rev. 1:14–17).

That day will be His day. Forever gone will be the mocking and jeering against Him. The Lamb has now returned as a Lion. The Lord Jesus will be "revealed from heaven with His mighty angels, in flaming fire taking vengeance on those who do not know God, and on those who do not obey the gospel of our Lord Jesus Christ. These shall be punished with everlasting destruction from the presence of the Lord and from the glory of His power, when He comes, in that Day, to be glorified in His saints and to be admired among all those who believe" (2 Thess. 1:7–10).

CORONATION DAY

That day is not just our coronation day. More importantly, it is His. Jesus Christ will be glorified in His saints. Then Christ's followers will begin their rule with Him. Here we talk of long-term and short-term investments. With heaven's rewards in mind, it is always sound to make spiritual long-term investments. The interest accrued on the principal is literally out of this world.

It is always wise to condition ourselves toward God-honoring living. And we should be just as dedicated in our spiritual workouts as athletes in training. For, in fact, we *are* in training—to rule over the nations in Christ's coming new world order. Then Jesus will reign, and those who qualify will reign with Him.

When describing eternal rewards, the Bible often refers to them as crowns. Interestingly, two Greek words are translated "crown." From one we get our word *diadem*. The use of this word is always reserved as a symbol of kingly or imperial dignity. It is this royal diadem with which Jesus Christ will one day be crowned as King of kings.[5]

A second Greek word for crown is *stephanos*. This is the word employed to describe the crowns for overcoming believers in Christ. These crowns are symbols of triumph. Scripture speaks of five crowns believers may win. Clear qualifications are given for each crown. To win these crowns is to have treasures in heaven. So living in such a way as to secure these symbols of triumph becomes a foundational motivation for living an overcoming life. It is to live for what matters forever, to live in heaven's honor. R. T. Kendall observes, "My reward in heaven (may God grant that there is such) will come *entirely* by whether I practiced what

I preached: walking in the light, dignifying the trial, totally forgiving others, and placing utmost priority on my intimacy with Him."[6]

The *crown of righteousness* is reserved for those who so love the hope of Christ's return that they have reordered their lives in light of His coming. This beautiful victor's crown is for those who have experienced the purifying effect of the imminent return of Christ.

When I was growing up, my mother had a tried and tested way of correcting my bad behavior. All she had to do was remind me, "Your father is coming soon." Believe me, it had a purifying effect! Just so, the prospect of the return of Christ at any moment has a sanctifying effect on the believer's life. The blessed hope of Christ's imminent return is a purgative in our lives. "And everyone who has this hope in Him purifies himself, just as He is pure" (1 John 3:3).

Sometimes the message of the Second Coming of Christ is used as an evangelistic warning to unbelievers. But the essential message the unbeliever must hear is of Christ's *first* coming, the biblical *kerugma* of His death and resurrection. The message of Christ's Second Coming is the blessed hope of the *believer*.[7] And it is contemplation of this glorious event that purifies and thus qualifies the believer to receive the crown of righteousness. As Paul approached the end of his life, he rejoiced, "I have fought the good fight, I have finished the race, I have kept the faith. Finally, there is laid up for me the crown of righteousness, which the Lord, the righteous Judge, will give me on that Day, and not to me only but also to all who have loved His appearing" (2 Tim. 4:7–8).

When Paul wrote these words to Timothy, he was awaiting his trial in Rome. Yet he was much less interested in his upcoming appearance before the high court of Rome than he was in his upcoming appearance at the judgment seat of Christ. Paul knew Caesar might not rule in his favor; the day the scales would truly balance would be when Paul stood before Christ.

Love for Jesus is the highest motive for serving Him. At least it should be. But most of us find that our motives are not fully sanctified at all times. For those of us still in the process of being changed from glory to glory, it doesn't hurt to remember that Jesus could return at any time. And certainly we want to be found serving Him with integrity when He comes. "Who then is that faithful and wise steward, whom his master will make ruler of his household...? Blessed is that servant whom his master will find so doing when he comes. Truly, I say to you that he will make him ruler over all that he has" (Luke 12:42–44). The scope of our future stewardship is determined by our faithfulness now. And our desire to be faithful is prodded by the knowledge that this may be the day He returns.

I remember well into the 1970s you could often see large crosses dotting the landscape on the sides of highways. Usually these words were painted on those crosses: *Prepare to meet thy God.* It may have been something of a gauge of the secularizing of America that these crosses began to quickly disappear about thirty years ago.

Now here we are in a new century, a new millennium. With each passing day we draw closer to the time when Jesus will split the skies. Yet ironically we seem to be hearing less about this wonderful, blessed hope. Some Christians seem content to set up an earthly kingdom that can exist equally well with or without the physical return of Christ. But this has not been the historic longing of the church. Yes, Christians have always longed for Christ's kingdom to come. But historically they have always tied the full coming of that kingdom with the coming of the King.

There were dual thrills that ran concurrently through the hearts of the early Christian believers. Any careful study of Scripture shows that the early church fully expected the physical return of Christ from heaven any day. Yet at the same time they made long-term plans on how to get the gospel to the farthest reaches of their known world. They were planting the kingdom while waiting for the rapture.

Why do we tend to see these two hopes as dichotomous? Is it because we, unlike the early church, have had twenty centuries to systematize our theology? Have we polarized hopes that God would have us view as a unified whole?

In any event, a righteous life is always in order for those who call themselves Christians. And the crown of righteousness awaits those who long for Christ's return—and live like it.

The requirement for the *crown of life* is to be faithful until death. "Do not fear any of those things which you are about to suffer," Jesus urged the church in Smyrna. "Be faithful until death, and I will give you the crown of life" (Rev. 2:10). He encourages His church today with the same promise. This victorious crown of life is reserved for those who serve the Lord well through suffering.

It is my privilege to often be among the leaders of the robust church in developing nations. They have learned to suffer for Christ with dignity and courage. By contrast, the Western Hemisphere church has not allowed for a theology of suffering. But we now live in a world where anyone who desires to be loyal to Jesus—no matter where he or she lives—must know what the Bible says about responding honorably to suffering and even martyrdom.

Often called the martyr's crown, the crown of life is also laid in store for those who give their last full sacrifice of devotion in furthering the gospel. One of my dearest friends, a Congolese pastor, was martyred for his courageous stand for Christ a few years ago. Men who have attended Global Advance's Frontline Shepherds Conferences have later paid with their lives for advancing the gospel. For each martyred believer, there is a victor's crown of life on the other side of their suffering.

There is no possibility of rectifying all the injustices that have assaulted suffering Christians from the perspective of this life alone. From the limited vantage point of this life, everything doesn't always add up, and good is not always rewarded in kind. It will take the judgment seat of Christ to properly honor battle-scarred followers of Christ who have faithfully lived for Him and seemingly received only more difficulties in this life as a result.

James encourages such faithful followers: "Blessed is the man who endures temptation; for when he has been proved, he will receive the crown of life which the Lord has promised to those who love Him" (James 1:12). Here the thought is carried beyond physical martyrdom. To die to self, whether this is expressed in actual death or other courageous sacrifice, qualifies you to receive this crown. James also describes the essence of what it really means to love Jesus. To love Jesus is to endure when we are tempted. In this verse he gives a spiritual equation: $A = B$ and $B = A$. The person who loves Christ is the one who endures temptation and vice versa. Unflinching devotion in the face of attack—that's the test of love's commitment.

The *incorruptible crown* is conferred on those who live disciplined lives as good soldiers of Jesus Christ. It is the heavenly, imperishable laurel given to winners in the greatest race of all—the race that is set before us as believers in Jesus. The writer of Hebrews reminds us that heaven's grandstands are filled with saintly spectators who cheer us on in this contest.[8] Since they are watching and, more importantly, since *He* is watching, we run with focus and perseverance.

To win this race we must be properly trained. And life sees to it that we go through spiritual drills far more grueling than stomach crunches and wind sprints. As with an athlete in training, we may be called upon to forgo even legitimate desires for a time to train as spiritual champions. There can be no true discipleship to Jesus without discipline. To put it bluntly, there are two pains that are set before you as a follower of Jesus. There is the pain of denying the control of the Holy Spirit and living instead for the flesh. Or there is the pain of denying the flesh and living instead under the control of the Spirit. One pain produces nothing but regret and a wasted life. The other pain produces an incorruptible crown.

The body's desires for food, rest, and sex are all legitimate and implanted by God. However, illicit acquiescence to any of these can become idolatry. We must bring even the legitimate cravings of the body under discipline, just as an athlete does when training for the big event. "Everyone who competes in the games goes into strict training. They do it to get a crown that will not last; but we do it to get a crown that will last forever" (1 Cor. 9:25, NIV). Paul cultivated a healthy fear of the Lord—and a deep concern that after he had preached to others he himself could be "disqualified for the prize" (1 Cor. 9:27, NIV). Paul was not dreading the possibility that he might lose his salvation. Instead he was ever mindful of the fearful possibility that he might forfeit eternal rewards by failing to fulfill God's purposes for his life.

The *crown of rejoicing* is fittingly named. This is the soulwinner's crown. It will be bestowed on those who love those who do not know Christ and prayerfully share His love with them by the example of their lives and their verbal witness.

Every believer in Jesus carries an evangelistic mandate, what is often called the Great Commission. Christ's mandate to go and make disciples of all the nations is incumbent upon all who have experienced a spiritual rebirth. As commissioned followers of Christ, we are in two groups: the few who are gifted as evangelists, and the vast majority who are to "do the work of an evangelist" (2 Tim. 4:5). Into whichever category you may fall, the commission is the same. We are mandated as believers to open our mouths and share the good news of Jesus Christ.

But just as we have discarded a theology of suffering, we also have left a "burden for the lost" out of our vocabulary and our experience. These great omissions have led the American church toward spiritual impoverishment. The psalmist said, "He who continually goes forth weeping, bearing seed for sowing, shall doubtless come again with rejoicing, bringing his sheaves with him" (Ps. 126:6). The Bible also teaches that the birth of spiritual children is preceded by the prayerful travail of God's people (Isa. 66:8).

It's true both physically and spiritually. Breathing exercises and prenatal classes notwithstanding, pain precedes physical birth. In the same way, somebody somewhere has to be burdened before children are born into the kingdom. That's why the soulwinner's crown is a crown of rejoicing; you have to do some weeping to get it.

Those who take this supreme command of our Lord seriously will, as a result, obey it. And for those who consistently seek to bring people to faith in Christ, a crown of rejoicing is reserved. God's Word promises, "Those who sow in tears shall reap in joy" (Ps. 126:5).

I cannot conceive of anything more joyful in all eternity than the sight of others in heaven that we have personally brought to faith in Christ. It will be just as Paul said: "For what is our hope, or joy, or crown of rejoicing? Is it not even you in the presence of our Lord Jesus Christ at His coming? For you are our glory and joy" (1 Thess. 2:19–20).

Let me ask you a pointed question. Will anyone be eternally grateful to you for your witness to them? Will anyone approach you in heaven and say, "I'm here because of you. Your love, prayers, and witness brought me to Christ"?

Finally, the *crown of glory* awaits those who have faithfully guided and shepherded the people of God. This crown is for those who feed the flock of God with prayerful diligence as pastors and church leaders. The hypocrisies of some spotlighted preachers tend to discredit all ministers of the gospel. This is a false indictment on many godly people who serve Christ nobly day in and day out. This crown also extends, in my opinion, to those who lift up the hands of their spiritual leaders in love, affirmation, and support. Jesus said, "He who receives a prophet in the name of a prophet shall receive a prophet's reward" (Matt. 10:41).

Peter describes the qualifications for this laurel of victory:

> To the elders among you, I appeal as a fellow elder, a witness of Christ's sufferings and one who also will share in the glory to be revealed: Be shepherds of God's flock that is under your care, serving as overseers—not because you must, but because you are willing, as God wants you to be; not greedy for money, but eager to serve; not lording it over those entrusted to you, but being examples to the flock. And

when the Chief Shepherd appears, you will receive the crown of glory
that will never fade away.

—1 Peter 5:1–4, niv

Many faithful pastors serve in situations that appear unsuccessful to natural eyes. Many serve the Lord honorably in obscure settings with seemingly little influence. But when Christ, the Chief Shepherd returns, these faithful "no-name" servants will be thrust into universal prominence. As the redeemed of all ages look on, the King of kings will confer His approval on them with a crown of glory.

CROWN HIM WITH MANY CROWNS

Do you desire these heavenly treasures? You should. Not because they indicate some level of spiritual achievement, but because Jesus says they're valuable and you will not want to be empty-handed before the Lord. Philip Yancey wrote, "For years all the New Testament talk about eternal rewards embarrassed me. Now, however, I see eternal rewards as the ultimate form of deferred gratification." What value are you placing on heaven's rewards? Yancey continues, "Jesus never seemed the least bit embarrassed about future rewards and punishment. Perhaps this is because he had lived on the other side and knew firsthand that what awaits us there merits any amount of deferred gratification here."[9]

It should go without saying that the purpose of these rewards is never to flaunt them. They will be symbols of victorious service in the previous sphere. They will also serve as something tangible and valuable we can lay at the feet of Jesus. True worship always involves giving. And nothing could be more thrilling and more soul satisfying than to have something in our hands of high value (as heaven measures worth) to offer in worship at the pierced feet of Jesus.

The Tower of London is the secure deposit for the priceless crown jewels of England. The dazzling brilliance of these regal crowns is literally breathtaking. The queen's Imperial Crown of State alone contains 2,783 diamonds, 277 pearls, 17 sapphires, 11 emeralds, and 5 rubies.[10]

This crown is as beautiful as it ever was, and its monetary worth keeps rising. Yet what this crown represents has been in rapid decline for sixty years. The formerly unrivaled British Empire continues to shrink in strength and influence. The crown still remains, but the kingdom itself is receding.

Queen Victoria (who ruled during the years of Britain's greatest reach and rule) understood well that all earthly kingdoms, including hers, must eventually bow and make way for the eternal kingdom of Jesus Christ. The hymn "The Day Thou Gavest, Lord, Is Ended" was specially chosen by Queen Victoria to be sung in every Anglican church on the occasion of her Diamond Jubilee celebration. John Ellerton had written the lyrics to be sung at missionary meetings. He was keenly aware of the Christian privilege and responsibility to take the gospel to the whole world. This hymn clearly expresses that global vision. It is a reminder that, while earthly kingdoms all finally contract and die, the kingdom of God will live forever. It is ever expanding, and the church of Jesus Christ is never sleeping.

> The day Thou gavest, Lord, is ended,
> The darkness falls at Thy behest;
> To Thee our morning hymns ascended,
> Thy praise shall sanctify our rest.
>
> We thank Thee that Thy church unsleeping,
> While earth rolls onward into light,
> Through all the world her watch is keeping,
> And rests not now by day or night.[11]

The eternal treasures we desire will never diminish in value, and they will forever represent a kingdom that will only grow mightier from age to age. "The kingdoms of this world [will] become the kingdom of our Lord and of His Christ, and He shall reign forever and ever!" (Rev. 11:15).

Whether these heavenly treasures are actual crowns (as we perceive crowns) is not even the point. What is important is that Jesus says there are real treasures in a real heaven, and we can store them up *there* in this life *here*. Whatever Jesus defines as "treasures," I define as treasures— timeless, nondiminishing, noncorrosive treasures. As magnificent as some of Earth's treasures are, they cannot be favorably compared to the immeasurable beauty and worth of heaven's treasures. "Eye has not seen, nor ear heard, nor have entered into the heart of man the things which God has prepared for those who love Him" (1 Cor. 2:9).

CHAPTER TWELVE

BUILT TO LAST

Let us hold fast the confession of our hope without wavering, for He who promised is faithful.

—HEBREWS 10:23

He has sounded forth the trumpet
That shall never sound retreat,
He is sifting out the hearts of men
Before His judgment seat.
O be swift, my soul, to answer Him!
Be jubilant, my feet!
Our God is marching on.[1]

—JULIA WARD HOWE

A FRIEND TOLD ME A TRAGIC STORY.

One night as he was driving home he saw a house on fire. Firefighters were just arriving and seemed helpless to prevent the home's rapid destruction to ash and cinder.

Across the street was the elderly couple who had lived in that home. My friend went over to offer words of encouragement. As he drew closer, he saw the wife rocking in a rocking chair staring blankly at the licking flames. Behind her stood her traumatized husband patting her on the shoulder with the same frozen gaze of fear.

You see, the loss of the house was the least of their worries. It seems this couple didn't like banks. Over their fifty years of marriage they had stashed away every spare dollar in a secret place inside their home, saving it "for a rainy day." What they did not count on was a night of fire. Now their entire life's savings were rising as worthless incense toward the sky. A lifetime of work—up in smoke.

UP IN SMOKE

As has already been stated, the Christian who lives to please himself jeopardizes any hope of treasures in heaven. He literally risks seeing his life go up in smoke when he stands before the Lord.

One of the fullest treatments in Scripture of the coming judgment of believers is given by the apostle Paul in this passage:

> For no one can lay any foundation other than the one already laid, which is Jesus Christ. If any man builds on this foundation using gold, silver, costly stones, wood, hay or straw, his work will be shown for what it is, because the Day will bring it to light. It will be revealed by fire, and the fire will test the quality of each man's work. If what he has built survives, he will receive a reward. If it is burned up, he will suffer loss; he himself will be saved, but only as one escaping through the flames.
>
> —1 CORINTHIANS 3:11–15, NIV

Paul is clear that if you're going to heaven at all, you must have the right foundation—the sure foundation of faith in Jesus Christ. Having established the correct foundation, Paul then appeals to us to build to last. To build with gold, silver, and precious stones is to live under the Holy Spirit's control, only for the glory of God. But it's also possible to build an unworthy edifice on the right foundation. It is possible to be a true Christian and build with perishable materials—wood, hay, or straw. We have two options as believers—we can build to last, or we can watch our lives and the hope of any rewards go up in smoke. That day—when we stand before Christ—will show the true quality of our works. It will bring to light the true quality of our works as they pass through the fires of God's holiness. Any dross will be burned up. Only what was built to last *will last*.

Our salvation is a gift of God's grace; it is explicitly *not* the result of any good deeds we have done. "For it is by grace you have been saved, through faith—and this not from yourselves, it is the gift of God—not by works, so that no one can boast" (Eph. 2:8–9, NIV). Yet the very next verse says that good works play a very important role in our lives as followers of Jesus. We engage in Christ-honoring deeds not in order *to be* saved but because we *are* saved. "For we are God's workmanship, created in Christ Jesus to do good works, which God prepared in advance for us to do" (Eph. 2:10, NIV).

So the judgment seat of Christ is not to determine whether or not you will be in heaven. Thank God, you will already be there if you have placed your faith in Jesus Christ. When you stand before the Lord, it will not be in judgment of your sins. Your sins have already been judged by being placed on Christ at the cross. Your sins are forever covered by His blood. This judgment of believers is not a judgment of sins. It is a judgment of our deeds and the motives behind them.

So instead of judging other Christians, we had better judge our own lives in preparation for His scrutiny of our every thought, word, deed, and motive. The fact that our sins will never be brought up against us is no license to sin. Any disobedience in our lives is deadly. The wages of sin is death for anybody—believer or unbeliever alike. Sin keeps us from serving the Lord acceptably, and this inevitably means a loss of reward.

This is well illustrated in the sad story of Lot in Genesis 18 and 19. Lot's uncle Abraham was a godly man. Lot, however, was not walking with the Lord and eventually lost his testimony, even with his own family. Judgment finally came. And while Lot was spared the fire and brimstone, everything he lived for was burned up. Lot himself was saved "yet so as through fire." But he was left with nothing.

The Greek word for "judgment seat" is *bema*. It was before the *bema* of Rome's supposed authority that Jesus was brought before Pilate. But it is before heaven's *bema* that Jesus will one day judge Pilate. It was before the *bema* in Caesarea that Paul made his defense before Felix. But it is before heaven's *bema* that Felix must make his defense to Christ. And it is before this *bema* that our lives will be scrutinized by the Lord Jesus—not, as with Pilate and Felix, to determine our salvation, but rather to determine what rewards, if any, we will receive.

There is a clear distinction between the nature and perhaps even the times of the judgments of believers and unbelievers. The Great White Throne Judgment is the judgment of unbelievers. The judgment seat of Christ is the judgment of believers' works. The Great White Throne Judgment is punitive, resulting in the expulsion of the unsaved from the presence of the Lord forever. The judgment seat of Christ is remunerative, resulting in eternal rewards for qualifying believers.[2]

It is important for us to keep this vital doctrine of coming judgment in balance, just as Scripture does. We must not tip the scales by teaching grace to the exclusion of the believer's accountability. Nor can we revert to any legalistic aberration of the gospel by suggesting that salvation is somehow earned through good works.

Christians have always had differences of opinion concerning the permanence of salvation. I have very decided views on this subject myself. However, that is not the subject of this book. For now we will leave it to the theologians to discuss if a Christian believer can fall from grace or if he is eternally secure.

But one thing is beyond dispute. Whether or not salvation may be lost, rewards certainly can be. The ground that has been gained spiritually must be guarded by continued obedience. Jesus encouraged the faithful church at Philadelphia, "Behold, I am coming quickly! Hold fast what you have, that no one may take your crown" (Rev. 3:11).

In *This Was Your Life*, the writers caution us to prepare for that day and guard the ground we have won for the next world: "When I stand before the Judgment Seat of Christ, I will stand there alone, unable to point to the failings of others. God will not hold me accountable for what others have done, only for what I have done. At the judgment 'every mouth [will] be stopped' (Rom. 3:19). There will be no excuses. No self-justification. No blame-shifting."[3]

Yes, it is possible even in heaven to *suffer loss.* That is why John warns us, "Look to yourselves, that we do not lose those things we worked for, but that we may receive a full reward" (2 John 8).

CROWN SNATCHERS

It's worth noting that Jesus says it is people—not experiences—that can snatch away our rewards. For behind painful circumstances inevitably there are people. It is relationships, good and bad, that affect our performance in any area. The following group of potential crown snatchers is not an exhaustive list, but it will show some of the results of faulty relationships that set us up for the loss of rewards.

Burnout is one early evidence of potentially lost rewards. One of the great schemes of the devil in our day is to wear down God's people. In my opinion, we are living in the day prophesied by Isaiah: "Even the youths shall faint and be weary, and the young men shall utterly fall" (Isa. 40:30). Excited young men and women, fresh out of Bible college or seminary, enter ministry brimming with hope and vision. Within a few years (sometimes a few months) they are demoralized and beaten. One reason is because our adversary the devil has picked up his pace of resistance and oppression. Spiritual warfare on a global scale has intensified. Every day we must remember to suit up for battle by putting on the whole armor of God.[4]

Another key factor in burnout is that supernatural ministry is often attempted in natural strength. We all need the anointing of the Holy Spirit to rise above the enemy's attacks. We must remember that our strength is from God Himself. "*He* gives power to the weak, and to those who have no might *He* increases strength" (Isa. 40:29, emphasis added). How then do we get this God-infused strength that bolsters us against burnout? The answer is clear: "Those who wait on the LORD shall renew their strength; they shall mount up with wings like eagles, they shall run and not be weary, they shall walk and not faint" (Isa. 40:31).

A great key to longevity in service for Christ is to keep our souls happy in the Lord. George Müller, who carried the heavy load of a large orphanage and other far-reaching ministries, understood this well. He said, "The first great and primary business to which I ought to attend every day was, to have my soul happy in the Lord."[5] Müller accomplished this by a mix each morning of worship, prayer, and devotional Bible reading. As an octogenarian he attributed his preservation to keeping a clear conscience before God and men; love of the Scriptures, which he had read through almost two hundred times; and the happiness he felt in God and His work.[6] This noted man of faith minimized his vulnerability to burnout by maintaining a clear conscience and a joyful heart.

The *trivia trap* also ensnares many today. Our penchant for nonstop entertainment snuggles up to us and whispers that we should wait until the proverbial "tomorrow" to seek what is really important. Tonight we need to relax. And before we know it, we have relaxed our way through an entire lifetime. The thousands of hours Christians spend in front of a television or computer screen merely for entertainment will surely come up for review when we stand before Jesus. Neil Postman was right when he observed, "America is the world's first culture in jeopardy of amusing itself to death."[7] And he wrote that more than twenty years ago! His words sting much deeper today.

Let's invest our time in what really matters. And things of true importance are exceedingly few. Os Guinness reminds us, "In a world dominated by the tyranny of time, the only final way to redeem the time is through the One who is the redeemer of everything."[8] What matters now and forever is glorifying God, loving God, and throwing our energies into the battle to make Him glorified and loved in our generation.

Because of the traumas of twenty-first-century living, many wish to insulate themselves from any more bad news. Disconnecting for a brief time to recharge spiritually and emotionally is healthy. Even Jesus did that. But prolonged, willful blindness to impending disaster by burying our heads in the sand is not smart; it's foolish. Those who sound warnings are often labeled alarmists. But aren't "alarmists" friends, not enemies, if their warnings can prevent destruction? Remember, Paul Revere was a hero. Those who may have been temporarily angered that he roused them from their sleep later thanked him for saving their lives.

So don't hide in some kind of noninvolvement. Esther toyed with this option until her uncle Mordecai reminded her that she could not hide her true identity just because she was in a privileged place. Esther was called by God to a great assignment, and so are you. So get in the game. Live with a biblical worldview. Live for God's glory. Live, and if need be, die in advancing Christ's kingdom. Don't choke on trivia!

If a ship is sinking, who is more truly benevolent—the guy passing out drugs to dull the panic or the guy passing out life jackets? Even if those drowning around us are angered by our attempts, we must keep yelling out warnings to come back to the lifeboats. And we must keep tossing life preservers in their direction. We dare not get caught in the trivia trap of noninvolvement. We are called to fulfill the Great Commission and bring kingdom transformation to our culture, our nation, and our world.

The twin villains of *disunity* and *disloyalty* are also rampant in our day. The renewal movement, which began in the 1960s in a unity perhaps unparalleled since the Reformation, is now seriously splintered. Unselfish deference has often devolved into ego empires.

I personally believe that a major agenda item of the Holy Spirit through the renewal movement was the spiritual unity of the church. This may have been of equal importance with the resurgence of spiritual gifts. Of course, the unity I'm speaking of is not organizational or man-made. In fact, I believe the unity sparked by the Holy Spirit renewal was God's counter to much of the liberal, man-induced unity based on compromise. God was producing a spiritual bonding, a unity that went past labels to a common commitment to Jesus as Lord. But much of that has now been jeopardized. For with the big blessings came big bucks. And with that came power maneuvers. And the unimpeded flow of the Spirit was at least partially blocked. We need to pray the prayer of the godly Scottish preacher Alexander Whyte, "We care not who is second, Lord, as long as Thou art first."

There is one crown snatcher that may be more deadly than any previously mentioned. It is the vicious villain of *bitterness*. Over the years I have watched this silent killer sideline many people. No wonder the writer of the letter to the Hebrews pleads, "Pursue peace with all people, and holiness, without which no one will see the Lord: looking diligently lest anyone fall short of the grace of God; lest any root of bitterness springing up cause trouble, and by this many become defiled" (Heb. 12:14–15).

May I get personal? What about you? Have you let a root of bitterness begin to choke your joys and hopes? Dwight Carlson writes, "Most people for whom bitterness is a major problem tend to be 'injustice-collectors.'"[9] Life sees to it that everybody has a story of injustice to tell. You have already been wronged in some way—and it won't be the last time. How you respond to the injustices of life makes all the difference in your fruitfulness now and your rewards then.

Bitterness is cancerous to the spirit. If unchecked, it can cancel out the good effects of years of service. I'm thinking now of several individuals who were household names among Christians ten or twenty years ago. Today they have become hardened, angry people living in self-made shells of isolation. Their former joy, anointing, and influence are all vanished. Unless we deal ruthlessly with bitterness, allowing the Lord to yank it out of us by the roots, our past influence will be neutralized and our future rewards will be jeopardized. David Hubbard reminded us, "The great danger in having enemies is not what they may do to us—it is what we do to ourselves as we allow harsh, bitter, angry reactions to develop."[10]

LIKE HIM

Instead of succumbing to the crown snatchers, we are to "make it our aim...to be well pleasing to Him" (2 Cor. 5:9). It is possible to be preserved blameless—body, soul, and spirit—to the coming of Christ.[11] If it were not possible, Paul would not have prayed for it. And even in an era when moral lapses seem to be the order of the day, God "is able to keep you from stumbling, and to present you faultless before the presence of His glory with exceeding joy" (Jude 24).

The mystery of worship is that the worshiper becomes like the object of his worship. Just think of the millions who worship gods of wood and stone. These false deities are incapable of hearing or perceiving. And many of those entrapped in such idolatry slowly become like the false gods they worship: unresponsive, indifferent, and impotent. Then consider the millions of religious zealots who, though they worship one almighty being, perceive him only as avenging and full of wrath. Once again, the worshiper is becoming like the perception of the one worshiped.

But biblically grounded followers of Christ are also destined to become like the object of their worship, Jesus Christ. With eyes focused on Him, we are being changed into His likeness "from glory to glory, just as by the Spirit of the Lord" (2 Cor. 3:18). We are destined to be like Him.

God has taken you on as a lifetime project. His one great objective is to conform you into the image of His Son. That is why there are no chance encounters in the life of a follower of Jesus. Each blow of life is designed to shape us more into the family likeness of Jesus Christ. "And we know that all things work together for good to those who love God, to those who are the called according to His purpose. For whom He foreknew, He also predestined to be conformed to the image of His Son" (Rom. 8:28–29).

This progressive conformity into the image of Jesus will continue until it is consummated in His return for us. When He comes, the very brilliance of His appearing will finish the process of changing us into

His likeness. "Beloved, now we are children of God; and it has not yet been revealed what we shall be, but we know that when He is revealed, we shall be like Him, for we shall see Him as He is" (1 John 3:2).

Like Him! That's your future. God has determined to take off all the rough edges. And when He's finished—and He *will* finish—you will look like Jesus. "Being confident of this very thing, that He who has begun a good work in you will complete it until the day of Jesus Christ" (Phil. 1:6).

PRAISE, HONOR, AND GLORY

The apostle Paul was an eternity-driven preacher. He wanted to see all those he influenced become mature in Jesus Christ. He knew this would bring them—and him—great joy when they would stand before Christ. That's why he implores us to always be "holding fast the word of life, so that I may rejoice in the day of Christ that I have not run in vain or labored in vain" (Phil. 2:16).

Jewel thieves and crown snatchers notwithstanding, a fantastic future awaits every Christian believer. My own study of this fascinating subject of rewards convinces me that all true believers will receive some level of affirmation from Jesus Christ when they stand before Him. This, in effect, is the minimal reward—loving affirmation from the Lord. At the same time that the counsels of the hearts are revealed, "each one's praise will come from God" (1 Cor. 4:5). Each individual believer has been born again to a living hope. That hope is our inheritance in heaven. Concerning the nature of this inheritance, Peter says it is incorruptible, undefiled, and lasting.[12] And this inheritance is, even as you read, already reserved in heaven for you.

Every believer in Christ will at least receive some level of praise from God. This is the portion of every child of God. But we are called to move into further realms of rewards; namely, honor and glory. "In this you greatly rejoice, though now for a little while, if need be, you have been grieved by various trials, that the genuineness of your faith, being much more precious than gold that perishes, though it is tested by fire, may be found to praise, honor, and glory at the revelation of Jesus Christ" (1 Pet. 1:6–7). I'm convinced "praise, honor, and glory" is not a redundancy. Rather, each may represent a level of heavenly rewards. While all believers will receive some praise at the judgment seat of Christ, those who have faithfully served Christ will be honored. Jesus promised as much when He said, "If anyone serves Me, him My Father will honor" (John 12:26).

But there is a higher level still. The Bible promises that those believers who have suffered for Christ will receive special glory from Him: "If you are reproached for the name of Christ, blessed are you, for the Spirit of glory and of God rests upon you" (1 Pet. 4:14). No doubt we will all be surprised in heaven when we see who's at the head of the line. Then, the last will be first. Those who have suffered and even died for Jesus Christ in obscurity will be thrust into eternal prominence. And many of today's highly visible "elite" will take a backseat to a new class of the uniquely glorious. This is one reason I try always to honor pastors from developing nations, praying grandmothers, and severely persecuted Christians. Heaven's new elite will include many of the disenfranchised of this world. Many of the dispossessed Christians of this age will reign with Christ and rule nations in the new heaven and the new earth.

The law of seedtime and harvest is in effect both in this life and the afterlife. This life serves as the planting time, and the future life brings harvest. The farmer must plant seeds if he expects a harvest. And the Christian must sow the seeds of righteousness now if he expects a harvest of rewards in eternity.

This very day you are earning the position of service you will hold in the coming time when Christ rules over a renovated, redeemed earth. In this life our most joyful and fruitful activities involve service for Jesus Christ. In the same way, our most thrilling experiences in Christ's coming kingdom will include administrating His program and purposes. We are building today for what will last forever. If Christians really understood this, they would surely be more motivated and focused in their service for Christ. They would live as if heaven matters.

Don't let anyone steal your reward. Build to last. Be a finisher, no matter how tough it may be. In 1968 a group of die-hard spectators remained in Mexico City's Olympic Stadium to see the final finishers of the Olympic marathon. More than an hour earlier Ethiopia's Mamo Wolde had broken the tape and won the race. But as the dwindling crowd waited for the final participants, it was getting cool and dark.

It seemed that the last runners were now finished, so the remaining spectators began to exit the stadium. Suddenly they heard the sounds of sirens and police whistles coming from the marathon gate into the stadium. As everyone watched, one lone runner made his way onto the track to finish the last lap of the twenty-six-mile race. It was John Stephen Akhwari from Tanzania. As he ran the 400-meter circuit, people could see that his leg was badly injured and bleeding. He had fallen and injured it during the race, but he didn't let the pain stop him. The remaining people in the stadium rose and applauded until he reached the finish line. As he hobbled away, Akhwari was asked why he didn't quit, having been injured and with no chance of winning a medal. "My country did not send me to Mexico City to start a race," he replied. "They sent me to finish the race."[13]

John Stephen Akhwari saw beyond the pain; he saw the finish line. John Akhwari finished his race. May you finish yours. Don't drop out. Endure the pain. For every genuine Christian believer, and certainly for those who serve or suffer, the best is yet to be.

CHAPTER THIRTEEN

Seeing the Invisible

It was by faith that Abraham obeyed when God called him to leave home and go to another land that God would give him as his inheritance. He went without knowing where he was going. And even when he reached the land God promised him, he lived there by faith—for he was like a foreigner, living in a tent....Abraham did this because he was confidently looking forward to a city with eternal foundations, a city designed and built by God.

—Hebrews 11:8–10, nlt

For three things I thank God every day of my life: thanks that He has vouchsafed me knowledge of His works; deep thanks that He has set in my darkness the lamp of faith; deep, deepest thanks that I have another life to look forward to—a life joyous with light and flowers and heavenly song.

—Helen Keller

"THE GREAT USE OF LIFE IS TO SPEND IT FOR SOMETHING THAT outlasts it." This observation by William James is especially true for followers of Jesus.

Unselfish service, fervent prayer, and the sacrificial investment of time and money yield immense blessings both to current and succeeding generations. C. S. Lewis was right when he noted, "If you read history you will find out that the Christians who did most for the present world were precisely those who thought most of the next."[1] To spend one's life for something that will outlast it is part of our innate longing for immortality.

We acknowledge, along with Scripture, that this life is merely a vapor that is here for a moment.[2] The mounting turbulence in our world underscores our vulnerability to sudden death via accidents, crime, fast-spreading pandemics, terrorist acts, or war. Yet something within us cries for some kind of continuance, some way of influencing things fifty or even a hundred years from now. One sure way to impact the future is through prayer. Just as there is no distance in prayer, there are no time limits in prayer. The prayers we offer to God now can and will affect the outcome of events yet future. We are to think, live, and pray toward the future.

This was dramatically illustrated in our lifetime with the dissolution of the old Soviet Union. When the Communist regime assumed power in 1917, Christians around the world began to pray. Seventy years passed before the back of this system was broken and the gospel once again began to spread freely throughout that nation and Eastern Europe. Finally, the accumulated might of believers' prayers won over evil. Suddenly, it happened. The silent pleas of millions of Christian throughout the cold war years for the breaking open of the iron curtain to the gospel were answered. Ann Graham Lotz notes, "There was no logical explanation for this dramatic series of events except that 'the bowls full of incense, which are the prayers of the saints,' had filled up! I wonder whose prayer was the last one to come in before God said, 'I have all I need in order to proceed to accomplish My purpose.'"[3]

THE WAY EVERLASTING

The Bible is replete with reminders that we are transients on our way to a more permanent city. As spiritual children of Abraham, like him, we too are looking "for a city which has foundations, whose builder and maker is God" (Heb. 11:10). We are to follow the model of those who live as if heaven matters. Self-styled existentialists who live only for the present and the material bring reproach to the name of Christ. In fact, Paul calls them enemies of the gospel. "Their destiny is destruction, their god is their stomach, and their glory is in their shame. Their mind is on earthly things. But our citizenship is in heaven" (Phil. 3:19–20, NIV). Paul then urges us to "stand firm in the Lord" (Phil. 4:1, NIV).

The choice is ours. We can adopt a self-absorbed hedonism and live only for the present, or we can live anchored by eternity's values. We can crater to the narcissistic lures of today, or we can live with a view to eternal compensations beyond our greatest dreams. We can pamper our whims, or we can invest in eternity. Either choice comes with consequences.

We are incessantly bombarded with all sorts of stimuli. All around us a myriad of voices clamor for our hearts and minds. Ours is a world of loud, impudent voices. The decibel levels of the twenty-first century are blaring at us with deafening volume. Our challenge today is to pull away from the "madding crowd's ignoble strife,"[4] quiet our hearts before God, and fine-tune our inner receptors to heaven's still, small voice.[5]

Coupled with the pressures of life today, these noises have spawned an epidemic of widespread anxiety. Yet every age has its own set of pressures. King David, for instance, felt the burden of keeping his nation righteous before God. In the midst of screaming urgencies David prayed not to lose sight of the eternal: "Lead me in the way everlasting," he prayed (Ps. 139:24). A Hebrew scholar told me this prayer could also be translated, "Lead me in the way of everlasting things."

If we are led in the way of everlasting things, we will reprioritize our schedules. A life given to everlasting things will give high priority to prayer. Prayer not only affects our current circumstances, but it also launches God's will into the future. Whatever your current status, you can leave a legacy of prayer that will bring untold blessings to those who follow you. Prayer always precedes God's intervention. Some are called to pray for an awakening they will see only from heaven's grandstands.

Their prayers in the present lay the groundwork for the Spirit's outpouring in the future.

The disciples were not chosen because of advanced spirituality over previous generations. They were simply blessed to live in the fullness of time for the Messiah to come. Jesus reminded them of their debt to the godly legacy of their predecessors when He said, "Many prophets and righteous men desired to see what you see, and did not see it, and to hear what you hear, and did not hear it" (Matt. 13:17).

We as well owe an immense debt to those who have gone before us. Our resources are much larger than in the past. Our access to technology and global travel contribute to making us a greatly advantaged generation. And because God is speeding up His work in the earth, we can accomplish His kingdom purposes more quickly than in the past. But this is precisely because of the godly lives and prayers of those who pioneered the way for us. If we are rising to greater heights in the Spirit, it is because we are standing on the shoulders of giants who have preceded us.

Everyone who reads this book will probably know the name Billy Graham. But few have heard of Pearl Goode. Yet, when we get to heaven we will likely find that a great deal of Mr. Graham's success was due to her.

When Billy Graham was beginning his large meetings in the early 1950s, this Methodist laywoman began to hear and read that God was raising up a new national evangelist. God impressed her to assist this young preacher, not so much with money as with prayer. She wrote to the Billy Graham offices and requested his itinerary. Then for the next several years, unknown to anyone, she would travel to the city where Mr. Graham was conducting evangelistic meetings, check into an inexpensive hotel, and lock the door. Throughout the days of the meetings she would stay in her room, pleading with God for souls and praying down God's power and blessings.[6] I'm looking forward to meeting Pearl Goode.

A life committed to everlasting things is committed to prayer. This brings benefit both to others and to us. It benefits our own era and generations to come. And it conditions us for our coming rule with Jesus Christ. Author Paul Billheimer believed that prevailing prayer in this life literally prepares us to rule with Christ in the age to come. He commented, "[The church] is...even now by virtue of the weapons of prayer and faith engaged in 'on-the-job' training for her place as co-sovereign with Christ over the entire universe following Satan's final destruction."[7]

A life given to everlasting things is also marked by praise and worship. Praise is the language of heaven. And if joy is "the serious business of heaven," as C. S. Lewis stated,[8] this joy is generated by worship of our perfect Redeemer-God. The Bible says that the praise and the worship of sincere believers are attractive and beautiful.[9] There is nothing quite so moving as honest praise and worship from a pure heart.

This is a powerful evangelistic tool as well. When unbelievers see honest-hearted Christians worshiping their God, something happens to them. The reality of the gospel may grip non-Christians through observing the church in worship more than through the most eloquent sermon. Someone has said that the church preaches to answer the questions raised by its worship. David said, "He has put a new song in my mouth—praise to our God; many will see it and fear, and will trust in the LORD" (Ps. 40:3). Our genuine praise to God often sparks conviction in the previously disinterested. Having seen God's glory through the power of praise and worship, they are convinced of their sin and need for God. Then they trust in the Lord. This sequence of evangelism all begins with a "new song" of praise to God.

If you follow the path of everlasting things, your life will be marked by prayer and praise. You will also put a high value on people. Relationships matter deeply to the eternity-oriented Christian. Very few things are eternal. According to the second law of thermodynamics, the earth itself is in a state of entropy; it is winding down, dying away. What's left when the planets themselves are gone?

God remains. His Word remains. And people remain. Every person you have ever known will live forever—somewhere. His or her destiny is either eternity with Christ or eternity without Him. So we should wrap arms of love around people, extending evangelistic warmth and compassion to unbelievers and nonpartisan fellowship and love to fellow Christians. In his classic sermon "The Weight of Glory," C. S. Lewis reminded his hearers that they were seated next to immortal beings. If for no other reason, we should honor each other and show dignity to people as eternal beings. We eat with, work with, disagree with, and experience life with immortal souls.

All of these components of an eternity-driven life—prayer, praise and worship, evangelism, kingdom building—these all prepare us for fruitful service for Christ both in this life and the next. Bruce Wilkinson reminds us, "In heaven we will desperately crave to serve. When we see our Savior, we will be swept up in a consuming, eternity-long desire to respond in love to Jesus—and worship and praise won't be enough. We will want to *do* something for Him."[10] If you hope to serve Him *then*, you'd better serve Him *now*.

A DEEPER PERCEPTION

For hundreds of years scientists viewed reality on the basis of Newtonian physics. Things were as they appeared to be: fixed and verifiable with nothing beyond. But with the advent of quantum mechanics and Einstein's theory of relativity, we envisioned new possibilities. Things may not be as bolted down as we had thought. Scientists are now conceding that there may be more to something than what we see, no matter how powerful the microscope or telescope.

Multiple realities may inhabit the same space. But only those with a deeper perception get glimpses of these other worlds. Elizabeth Barrett Browning understood this when she noted:

> ...Earth's crammed with heaven,
> And every common bush afire with God;

But only he who sees takes off his shoes;
The rest sit round it and pluck blackberries.[11]

You are standing (or sitting) on holy ground—right now. God is permeating the airport terminal or coffee shop or room where you're reading this—right now. "But only he who sees takes off his shoes." Those who see only with natural eyes sit in close proximity to God's presence, but, unaware of His presence, they just "pluck blackberries." Their lives are mundane though God's glory is all around them. They don't perceive Him. If we fail to see the deeper reality, we will walk right past what could have been blazing encounters with God. Though Earth is crammed with heaven, we often don't see it. In a spiritual stupor we just sit round and channel surf. The difference between a life brimming with purpose and a life of plucking blackberries is encountering the presence of God.

How deep is your perception? Do you see only with natural eyes? Elisha's servant was petrified as he looked on the horizon. What he saw was enough to scare anybody: he and Elisha were surrounded by bloodthirsty foreign soldiers. The prophet encouraged his servant with the incredible words that "those who are with us are more than those who are with them."

Yet how could that possibly be? Weren't their enemies breathing down their necks? But then Elisha prayed, "LORD, I pray, open his eyes that he may see." Immediately the servant saw that the enemy army surrounding them was itself surrounded by heaven's superior forces and chariots of fire.[12]

What a strange prayer—"that he may see." Didn't the servant already see? He saw well indeed, well enough to see the problem. But he did not see well enough to see the solution. He needed a deeper perception. And this new way of seeing melted his fear.

We're living in the very time prophesied by Jesus—"men's hearts failing them from fear and the expectation of those things which are coming on the earth" (Luke 21:26). Unspeakable acts of terror are a constant threat. But Jesus said that the antidote to fear is to look up—to have a deeper perception—because our redemption is near.[13]

Too many believers are overly fascinated with Satan's power. They are constantly seeing the activity of demons. But this is no great achievement. Even Elisha's nearsighted servant, through no special spiritual endowment, was able to see the enemies of the Lord. They were obviously there, right in front of him.

Frankly, it takes no rare insight to realize that Satan and his demonic hosts are poised to do battle against us. So I have a question for those who "see a demon behind every bush." Do you see the *angels* behind them? Only one-third of the angelic hosts fell through rebellion. They now constitute the demonic forces. But that means there are still two angels for every demon! It brings no comfort to a threatened church to announce that demons are poised to attack. What we need is keener spiritual eyesight, a deeper perception. We must see the far more numerous heavenly armies of the Lord who are even now ambushing hell's schemes!

If you can see the invisible, you will be strengthened to endure the tangible. Moses "endured as seeing Him who is invisible" (Heb. 11:27). So can you. There are three trademarks of a person with an eternal perspective. First, he or she *sees the invisible.* Such a person views life through the lens of eternity. He has two sets of eyes—natural eyes to see the material and spiritual eyes to see the eternal. And it's this second set of eyes that allows us to give true depth to what we see with our physical eyes. God is ready now to give you a deeper perception.

Following close on the heels of heightened spiritual sight is more highly sensitized hearing. This will require that we shut out the louder noises of the world. Just as dogs are keenly sensitive to pitches humans can't hear, so the eternity-oriented believer hears what others do not. Not only does he see the invisible, but *he also hears the inaudible.* We've heard what every other voice has to say. Many today get their theology in silly sound bites from late-night comedians. Now it is time to "hear what *the Spirit* is saying to the churches."[14]

Some in the secular media have had a heyday attacking those who say God speaks to them. Even some professing Christians have joined the crowd of skeptics. Recently a joyful Christian was asked incredulously, "You mean you hear God speak to you?" With a smile she replied, "You mean you *don't*?" If someone does not hear Jesus, it may well be because he does not belong to Him, for Jesus said, "My sheep hear My voice" (John 10:27).

Does this mean we should expect to hear an audible voice? Not usually. It's much louder than that! For the sensitized believer, the Spirit's inaudible voice in his or her spirit is much more pronounced than the voices of those around him. In the past, an ear tuned to heaven was valuable. But in our day it is more than valuable; it is vital. Today's followers of Jesus are learning to literally live "by every word that proceeds from the mouth of God" (Matt. 4:4). With each passing year it is increasingly vital for believers to live by revelation.

This does not undercut the authority of the written Word in any way. I believe strongly in the inerrancy of Scripture. But I do not believe that God became mute and His people became deaf the day the Canon of Scripture was closed. God is still speaking. And His people are still hearing.

We are at the changing of the guard. The baton of the church's leadership is being passed to a new generation. But it is not merely being transferred from older to younger. There is a new breed of leaders coming on the scene. A new generation of "Samuels" are beginning to lead. The young Samuel could hear what the aging priest could not.[15] There was an increase in perception.

Jesus pronounced loving yet firm warnings to His churches in Revelation 2 and 3. Then He said, "He who has an ear, let him hear what the Spirit is saying to the churches." In the midst of our spiritual family's dirty laundry that has been exhibited gleefully by our critics, the

Spirit is speaking again to the churches. If we dismiss these last few convulsive years as merely the devil's attacks against us, I submit that we're not hearing very well. God wants the church's attention. And once we're stilled before Him, He has plenty to say to us. "He who has an ear, let him hear."

Those who see the invisible and hear the inaudible will consequently *embrace the imperishable.* Look about you. Everything can be neatly placed into two categories: perishable and imperishable. Almost everything we see with physical eyes is in the first category. And God knows we need to get rid of a lot of perishable clutter. That's why He's shaking things up.

> The phrase "one last shaking" means a thorough housecleaning, getting rid of all the historical and religious junk so that the unshakable essentials stand clear and uncluttered. Do you see what we've got? An unshakable kingdom! And do you see how thankful we must be? Not only thankful, but brimming with worship, deeply reverent before God. For God is not an indifferent bystander. He's actively cleaning house, torching all that needs to burn, and he won't quit until it's all cleansed. God himself is Fire!
>
> —HEBREWS 12:27–29, THE MESSAGE

What about the earth itself? Scripture teaches it will be purged with fire. How about wealth? It takes wings and flies away. Health, maybe? Not a chance; the outward man perishes. What about our expensive clothes? Not to mention the fact that they will soon be as outdated as polyester leisure suits; moths invade them. Cars? Rust corrodes them. Houses? Thieves break in and steal. And now thieves are breaking into your very identity by hacking into your own computer.

So what's left?

Treasures in heaven.

These treasures are not only inanimate rewards, such as crowns. The treasures are people themselves. Paul told the Thessalonian church, "For what is our hope, or joy, or crown of rejoicing? Is it not even you in the presence of our Lord Jesus Christ at His coming? For you are our glory and joy" (1 Thess. 2:19–20). What is our glory and joy? Not things—people. To have people we love with us in heaven—this is our hope, our joy, our crown of rejoicing. To embrace the imperishable is to embrace people. And to embrace the imperishable is to embrace our Father God. The highest of all rewards is to know God. God reminded Abram that He, not His blessings, was the grand prize: "I am your shield, your exceedingly great reward" (Gen. 15:1). A right relationship to God and a right relationship to people—these are the greatest rewards in this life and the next.

ANOINTED TO SERVE

One of Stonewall Jackson's maxims was, "If you want to be more heavenly minded, think more of the things of heaven and less of the things of earth."[16] It is the "otherworldly" who are best prepared and most quickly prompted to get this world's dirt under their nails and effect real change. Don't ever buy the trite little adage about "being so heavenly minded you're no earthly good." It is precisely the heavenly minded who are the uniquely anointed to serve their generation.

Those who see the invisible, hear the inaudible, and embrace the imperishable can *do the impossible*! Spiritual perception requires faith. Without faith most everything you might attempt will prove impossible, including being pleasing to God.[17] But Jesus said, "If you can believe, all things are possible to him who believes" (Mark 9:23). Do you have faith to see the invisible? Will you believe to hear the inaudible? Have you chosen to embrace the imperishable? Then you are poised to do the impossible.

Simple godly living, as demonstrated by the characteristics just mentioned, brings thrilling results. Not only will you be blessed, but your descendents will also be blessed. "He who fears the LORD has a secure fortress, and for his children it will be a refuge" (Prov. 14:26, NIV).

A godly life blesses society as well. This is vividly pictured in an interesting bit of research into the lives of two men, Max Jukes and Jonathan Edwards. Max Jukes was a vocal atheist who lived a dishonorable life. He married an ungodly woman. Among the descendants of this union, 310 died as paupers, 150 were criminals, 7 were murderers, 100 were alcoholics, and more than half of the women were prostitutes. His 540 descendants cost the state one and a quarter million dollars.

During the same time that Max Jukes lived, there lived a great man of God, Jonathan Edwards. He was instrumental in igniting America's first large-scale revival, the Great Awakening. Edwards married a godly woman. An investigation was made of more than thirteen hundred of their descendants. Among them were thirteen college presidents, sixty-five college professors, three United States senators, thirty judges, one hundred lawyers, sixty physicians, seventy-five military officers, one hundred pastors and missionaries, sixty authors, one vice president of the United States, and eighty public officials in other capacities. There were also governors of states and ambassadors to other countries. His descendants did not cost the government a penny.[18] "The memory of the righteous is blessed" (Prov. 10:7).

On this short stopover on our way to forever, Jesus said His followers are the salt of the earth.[19] Salt may sting, but it also heals, preserves, and makes people thirsty. Our influence, though sometimes a sting to the open sores of society, should be a preservative and make people thirst for Jesus Christ, the living water.

While our nihilistic culture pursues selfish indulgence, it is in the same breath pleading with us, "Pass the salt!" The world expects the church—and is *begging* the church—to be salt to an insipid generation and light to a darkened culture. As E. M. Bounds noted, "The great need of the church in this and all ages is men [and women] of such commanding faith, of such unsullied holiness, of such marked spiritual vigor and consuming zeal, that their prayers, faith, lives and ministries will be of such a radical and aggressive form as to work spiritual revolutions which will form eras in individual and church life."[20]

To Lay Ourselves Out

I try to be a student of those who die well, men and women who gave the last ounces of their strength in heaven's honor. I've wanted to learn not only from their sacrificial lives but also from the days leading up to their promotions to heaven. A voice from heaven assures us, "'Blessed are the dead who die in the Lord from now on.' 'Yes,' says the Spirit, 'that they may rest from their labors, and their works follow them'" (Rev. 14:13).

More than a decade ago Princess Diana's untimely death overshadowed the death that same week of Mother Teresa. Yet an entire nation—a Hindu nation—afforded this humble Christian nun a state funeral and highest honors. (It's worth noting that there has been a dramatic turning to Christ by millions in India since Mother Teresa's death.)

Until her final days Mother Teresa was still working to relieve the plight of suffering humanity and bring God's love and His kingdom realities to some of the most disaffected people on earth. Interestingly, the closer she got to heaven, the more involved she became in meeting needs here on Earth. The more she suffered physically, the more she fought to alleviate the suffering of others.

Mother Teresa was fortified internally, even as her body was wasting away. She saw the finish line, and she saw beyond the finish line to that day. In *Words to Live By* she wrote, "At the end of our lives, we will not be judged by how many diplomas we have received, how much money we have made or how many great things we have done. We will be judged by 'I was hungry and you gave me to eat. I was naked and you clothed me, I was homeless and you took me in.' ... This is Christ in distressing disguise."[21]

At age eighty-two and almost blind, William Booth, founder of The

Salvation Army, gave these last public words before ten thousand people assembled at Royal Albert Hall in London:

> While women weep, as they do now, I'll fight; while children go hungry, as they do now, I'll fight; while men go to prison, in and out, I'll fight; while there is a drunkard left, while there is a poor lost girl upon the streets, while there remains one dark soul without the light of God, I'll fight—I'll fight to the very end.[22]

William Carey, a prime mover of the modern missions movement, believed good works done for God's glory are the seed and heaven's rewards are the harvest. On his deathbed Carey said to a friend, "When I am gone, say nothing of me; speak about Dr. Carey's Savior." He wrote:

> We are exhorted "to lay up treasures in heaven." . . . It is also declared that "whatsoever a man soweth, that shall he also reap." These Scriptures teach us that the enjoyments of the life to come bear a near relation to that which now is; a relation similar to that of the harvest and the seed. It is true all the reward is of mere grace, but it is nevertheless encouraging; what a "treasure," what a "harvest" must await such characters as Paul, and Eliot and Brainerd [early missionaries to Native Americans John Eliot and David Brainerd], and others, who have given themselves wholly to the work of the Lord. What a heaven will it be to see the many myriads of poor heathens, of Britons amongst the rest, who by their labors have been brought to the knowledge of God. Surely a "crown of rejoicing" like this is worth aspiring to. Surely it is worthwhile to lay ourselves out with all our might, in promoting the cause and the kingdom of Christ.[23]

In my lifetime, perhaps no one "laid himself out" in promoting the cause and kingdom of Christ more than Bill Bright. He was prolific throughout his life as the visionary founder of Campus Crusade for Christ, the author of the gospel tract "The Four Spiritual Laws" and the primary fund-raiser for the single greatest evangelistic tool of the twentieth century, the *JESUS* film.

As his body was increasingly ravaged with pulmonary fibrosis and he fought for every breath, he remained totally engaged in reaching people for Jesus Christ. Often he would literally go from the oxygen tank to the studio to capture one more session. Then it was back to the oxygen tank. During the last two years of his life, although much of the time he was confined to bed, he was involved in some eighty projects designed to bring people to faith in Christ and train them as His disciples. Shortly before Dr. Bright's death he wrote, "I respect all the profound theological propositions one can, and probably should, absorb; but right now, if it does not pertain plainly to life or death, heaven or hell, and the fulfillment of the Great Commission, my interest is short-lived."[24]

In reviewing his life, Dr. Bright observed, "Regrets? If I had my life to live over, I would have trusted Christ sooner and sought to have the faith to recruit and train more Spirit-filled followers of Jesus to help fulfill the Great Commission."[25]

What strikes me about all these heaven-bound believers is that they lived and died as if heaven matters. They didn't mentally or emotionally check out until they checked in at their final, permanent address. These heavenly minded pioneers were building and extending Christ's kingdom until the very moment they stepped into eternity. All my study for this book convinces me they are still working for Jesus. They're not bored, and they're not endlessly strumming harps. These spiritual activists are still *active*.

As their eyesight dimmed they saw the invisible more clearly. As their hearing weakened they picked up heaven's signals with greater clarity. They saw the invisible, heard the inaudible, and embraced the imperishable. And when we review their magnificent lives, we realize they did what was humanly impossible. They exited Earth strong in spirit, happy, and brimming with hope—solid, immovable, biblical hope. Faith, hope, and love—these three remained.

What a legacy.

CHAPTER FOURTEEN

A THEOLOGY OF HOPE

Blessed be the God and Father of our Lord Jesus Christ, who according to His abundant mercy has begotten us again to a living hope through the resurrection of Jesus Christ from the dead, to an inheritance incorruptible and undefiled and that does not fade away, reserved in heaven for you.

—1 PETER 1:3–4

And if I sing let me sing for the joy
That has born in me these songs,
And if I weep let it be as a man
Who is longing for his home.[1]

—RICH MULLINS

HAVE YOU EVER WONDERED WHY NEW CHRISTIANS SEEM invariably drawn to the most challenging book in the Bible to properly interpret—the Book of the Revelation?

This has always intrigued me. Several times I've urged a new believer to begin reading the Bible starting with John or Romans, only to have him ask, "But what about that book at the back of the Bible?" Why are they so fascinated with Revelation?

Years ago Pastor Jerry Cook asked the same question. He relates how he thought the devil was trying to confuse new believers by drowning them in charts, dates, numbers, and speculations about beasts and dragons. Why this desire at the very outset to dive into the deep end and read Revelation? Then the thought came to him: "Don't you think that desire may be born of the Holy Spirit?" The Lord impressed this pastor simply to read the Book of Revelation to his congregation and cautioned him, "Don't you dare do an exposition on it." Pastor Cook relates what happened:

> We simply read Revelation. When we got through we had a phenomenal concept of the *power of Jesus*, of the *sovereignty of God*, of the *security that is ours* on this planet, and of the utter, complete, unquestionable *triumph of the church* of Jesus Christ. On that...night the congregation stood together with uplifted hands and praised the Lord for nearly half an hour. I've never seen anything so powerful in all my life. I thought, *That's why the Lord takes new Christians to the Book of Revelation. What does a new Christian need to know more than those four things?*[2]

CHRIST OUR HOPE

In a word, new Christians want to know they have bought into *a sure hope*. And they have. Before we came to faith in Christ we were "without Christ...having no hope and without God in the world" (Eph. 2:12). Then Jesus changed everything. "But now in Christ Jesus you who once were far off have been brought near by the blood of Christ. For He Himself is our peace" (vv. 13–14).

Because of Jesus, we have peace. Yet many people today live with fear as their relentless companion. With the proliferation of weapons of mass destruction—along with the growing millions who would love to detonate them—many have literally lost hope. They face the future with dread instead of hope. The result is often a free fall into nihilism. Struggling through what seems a hopeless, senseless life, all that is left is to party on until disaster strikes.

Strangely, as our safety has become increasingly tenuous, a curious, widespread silence has enveloped much of the church on the very issues designed to bring us hope—the hope of the return of Christ, the hope of the rule of Christ, and the hope of heaven. Ted Dekker laments, "The gravest concern we now face is the fact that our *hope* for the afterlife has slipped into slumber. Our hope for heaven has fallen asleep. And when I say heaven, I mean Christ in heaven, for he is the Light of heaven, of the afterlife, of all the glory that awaits us."[3]

We have traded rock-solid, biblical hope for fragile, humanistic optimism. Believe me, they are *not* the same. Clear, scriptural teaching on our incontrovertible hope in Christ has too often been replaced with little homilies that basically say, "Hang in there! It's gonna get better." We have traded gold for fool's gold.

Let's get real. Tomorrow things could indeed get better, or tomorrow things could get much worse. The odds of a nuclear holocaust are spiking. We all face the very real potential of being victims of acts of terrorism. But if you know your Bible—and if you know your Savior—this does not mean you sink into a morose pessimism. On the contrary, it means you live in joy, confidence, and victory *no matter what may come.*

Terrorists may have their short day, *but they do not own the future.* The future belongs to Jesus Christ and His church! Your times are not in the hands of terrorists; your times are in the hands of the Lord.[4] The world is not headed for unending chaos. The world is headed toward an unshakable, glorious kingdom—the eternal kingdom of God.

When the Bible speaks of hope, it simply means we know God will make good on His promises. Jack Hayford explains that we have hope "not in the sense of an optimistic outlook or wishful thinking without any foundation, but in the sense of confident expectation based on solid certainty. Biblical hope rests on God's promises, particularly those pertaining to Christ's return. So certain is the future of the redeemed that the New Testament sometimes speaks of future events in the past tense, as though they were already accomplished. Hope is never inferior to faith, but is an extension of faith. Faith is for the present possession of grace; hope is confidence in grace's future accomplishment."[5]

The Bible is teeming with hope for those who put their trust in Christ:

Be joyful in hope, patient in affliction, faithful in prayer.

—ROMANS 12:12, NIV

I pray also that the eyes of your heart may be enlightened in order that you may know the hope to which he has called you, the riches of his glorious inheritance in the saints.

—EPHESIANS 1:18, NIV

We give thanks to the God and Father of our Lord Jesus Christ, praying always for you, since we heard of your faith in Christ Jesus and of your love for all the saints; because of the hope which is laid up for you in heaven, of which you heard before in the word of the truth of the gospel.

—COLOSSIANS 1:3–5

The knowledge of the truth that leads to godliness—a faith and knowledge resting on the hope of eternal life, which God, who does not lie, promised before the beginning of time.

—TITUS 1:1–2, NIV

We know that when He is revealed, we shall be like Him, for we shall see Him as He is. And everyone who has this hope in Him purifies himself, just as He is pure.

—1 JOHN 3:2–3

I want to be very clear. *Christ* is our hope. His return, His rule, His global glory—this is our hope. No Jesus—no hope. With Jesus—great hope. All our hope is wrapped up in Christ. He is "the Lord Jesus Christ, our hope" (1 Tim. 1:1). Through Christ we have:

- *Hope that He will come again.* "Looking for the blessed hope and glorious appearing of our great God and Savior Jesus Christ" (Titus 2:13).

- *Hope for a glorified body fit for eternity.* He "will transform our lowly body that it may be conformed to His glorious body, according to the working by which He is able even to subdue all things to Himself" (Phil. 3:21).

- *Hope of a home in heaven.* "In My Father's house are many mansions; if it were not so, I would have told you. I go to prepare a place for you. And if I go and prepare a place for you, I will come again and receive you to Myself; that where I am, there you may be also" (John 14:2–3).

- *Hope that the scales of justice will finally and forever be balanced.* God "has appointed a day on which He will judge the world in righteousness by the Man whom He has ordained. He has given assurance of this to all by raising Him from the dead" (Acts 17:31).

- *Hope that we will be reunited with loved ones already with the Lord.* "For the Lord Himself will descend from heaven with a shout, with the voice of an archangel, and with the trumpet of God. And the dead in Christ will rise first. Then we who are alive and remain shall be caught up together with them in the clouds to meet the Lord in the air. And thus we shall always be with the Lord" (1 Thess. 4:16–17).

- *Hope for the unrivaled reign of Jesus Christ over all the earth.* "The kingdoms of this world have become the kingdoms of our Lord and of His Christ, and He shall reign forever and ever!" (Rev. 11:15).

- *Hope of a new heaven and a new earth.* "Now I saw a new heaven and a new earth, for the first heaven and the first earth had passed away" (Rev. 21:1).

It's *all* because of Jesus. "Christ *in you* bringing with him the hope [assurance] of all the glorious things to come" (Col. 1:27, PHILLIPS). No wonder the great hymn writer Fanny Crosby exclaimed:

> Blessed assurance, Jesus is mine!
> Oh, what a foretaste of glory divine![6]

Your fellowship with Jesus today is a literal "foretaste of glory divine."

Paul summed it up well as he brought his letter to the church at Rome to a close. He had just assured them from many scriptures that God's promised Messiah would bring hope to the nations. This Seed of Jesse (Jesus Christ) would ultimately conquer all His enemies and restore His corrupted creation to its original splendor and purpose. Then Paul urged these early Christians to put full confidence in the coming triumph of Christ and His kingdom. Remember, these committed followers of Jesus were feeling the full heat of pagan Rome. Living in the capital of the empire, they knew that at any moment their faith in Christ could be put to the ultimate test. Paul was writing to people whose friends had been fed to lions or whose bodies had become flaming torches for Nero's garden parties—all because of their loyalty and love for Jesus. Paul wanted these Roman believers to know that one day Christ would crush not only the Roman Empire but also every human kingdom that defies His rule.

That same assurance buoys us today. If you look at events with only a temporal lens, it seems the church is losing and heaven's interests are being smothered by man's agendas. But if you view things with an eternal lens, today's discouraging snapshot yields to a beautiful love story culminating with Jesus as the great kinsman-redeemer and His church as His bride.[7] Trusting that Jesus will one day reign over the earth and that we will reign with him, our lives can be flooded with joy, peace, and faith. "May the God of hope fill you with all joy and peace as you trust in him, so that you may overflow with hope by the power of the Holy Spirit" (Rom. 15:13, NIV).

This I Know

Unspeakable pain can be endured, provided you have inside information regarding the ultimate outcome. Do you remember Job? He lost his wealth, position, health, and family—all in a single day. His pain was exacerbated by heartless "comforters" and a heartbroken, embittered companion. Anyone who has ever experienced heartaches and reversals (and that will probably be every person who picks up this book) can learn from Job's response in the midst of sudden disaster.

If, like Job, you were to lose everything you hold dear in a short amount of time—trust me, your theology would be up for review. And that's what happened to Job. Through much of the book that bears his name we find him processing through the pain. He asks the big questions of life. He wants to know, "Why do bad things happen to good people?" And then Job finally gets down to the bottom line.

What is left of faith when it is distilled to its essence? Job, having been stripped of almost everything he valued, was left with just one possession: a no-nonsense, no-hype faith in his Redeemer. After the devil had done his worst, Job discovered that at his very core he still retained a theology of hope. Despite his compounded tragedies he made a ringing confession of faith. He declared, "I know that my Redeemer lives, and He shall stand at last on the earth; and after my skin is destroyed, this I know, that in my flesh I shall see God" (Job 19:25–26).

When Jesus burst out of that tomb, your destiny and mine were forever changed. Our chains fell off! Death no longer gets the final word. His resurrection guarantees yours. "Because I live," Jesus promised, "you will live also" (John 14:19).

Job knew he had a living Redeemer who would one day stand on the earth in triumphant splendor. He saw beyond his present pain to a day free from all suffering. Job also knew that he would experience a physical resurrection. "In my flesh," he said, "I shall see God." The final destiny of his body was not corruption but a glorified body capable of enjoying God's presence forever. No trial is too difficult if you really know that, when all is said and done, you will see God and He will see you. This is a theology of hope.

Perhaps, like Job, you live and work in surroundings hostile to your faith in a living Redeemer. Your friends may be less than supportive. There may be angry denunciations of your stand for Christ even within your own family. You may feel like you've been pelted all at once with some of hell's heaviest arsenals. In such times, when faith is boiled down to what you know without question, your heart can be at rest with a confident assurance. You still have a triumphant, living Redeemer. He will write the final chapter. And in a body fashioned to dwell with Him forever you will see God.

Your Redeemer lives! He is your hope. David Bryant writes, "[Christ] is our all, now, because He is all supreme now. That makes Him our one great hope—*now*—just as fully as He will be at the End. To our happy surprise, the everlasting destiny of our lives throughout all the ages is linked inseparably to the very Person who actively reigns in our lives *today*."[8]

> For everything, absolutely everything, above and below, visible and invisible, rank after rank after rank of angels—*everything* got started in him and finds its purpose in him. He was there before any of it came into existence and holds it all together right up to this moment.... He was supreme in the beginning, and—leading in the resurrection parade—he is supreme in the end. From beginning to end he's there, towering far above everything, everyone.
> —COLOSSIANS 1:16–18, THE MESSAGE, EMPHASIS ADDED

So live as if heaven matters! Put Jesus at the center of your "world" because He *is* at the center of the entire universe. In an age dizzy with disasters and drunk with dread, we can live joyful, hope-filled lives because He lives.

TAKING OTHERS WITH YOU

A book *about* heaven that didn't challenge readers to get people *into* heaven would be seriously flawed. I cannot end this book without appealing to the church to restore evangelism as a high priority. In what must be one of the most tragic ironies of our time, as interest in spiritual matters has increased dramatically in our nation over the last several years, evangelism has waned. The church has grown weak in reaching people with the gospel precisely because we have not lived as if heaven—or hell—matters. Yet they could not matter more. Eternal destinies are at stake.

Again, I wish to be clear and true to Scripture. A life fit for heaven comes only and exclusively through establishing and cultivating a personal relationship with Jesus Christ. The only way to experience forgiveness of sins, eternal life, and a home in heaven is through faith in Him.[9] With Jesus, people go to heaven and are forever with the Lord. Without Jesus, they are separated from God forever in a horrible place the Bible calls hell. I agree with John Piper's assessment of our post-9/11 call as followers of Jesus. He writes, "Since September 11, 2001, I have seen more clearly than ever how essential it is to exult explicitly in the excellence of Christ crucified for sinners and risen from the dead. Christ must be explicit in all our God-talk."[10]

Our screaming need is to get a biblical worldview and a biblical world vision. We have a great, global challenge, and we serve Christ under His Great Commission.[11] Our task is to ensure that the gospel gets to every person on earth and that there is a Christ-exalting church among every people group on earth. We cannot hope to see this colossal challenge fulfilled without the empowering of the Holy Spirit. The *only* Christian discipline we can accomplish better on Earth than in heaven is sharing our faith in Christ with others. As a friend of mine once remarked, "The most important thing in life is ensuring that you are going to heaven. The second most important thing is taking other people with you."

This is what Paul had in mind when he envisioned his arrival in heaven and his appearance before Christ. He wrote that he wanted to present entire nations to Jesus as an offering of worship, sanctified by the Holy Spirit.[12] With the apostle Paul, when I get to heaven I don't just want to say, "Lord, here I am." I want to say, "Lord, here I am—and here are all these people I brought with me!"

God's design in world history is that redeemed people from all tribes, languages, and nations will one day lavishly worship Jesus as their Lord and God. As Paul put it in Romans 15:9, "that the Gentiles might glorify God for His mercy." God's intent among all the earth's ethnicities is "to take out of them a people for His name" (Acts 15:14).

And that's where we come in. After Jesus paid for our sins on the cross and rose from the dead, He ascended into heaven and sat down at the right hand of God the Father.[13] Christ sat down, indicating that His redemptive work was finished. In fact, those were His very words on the cross just before He commended His spirit to His Father—"It is finished!" (John 19:30). Now that His work is finished, ours has begun. World-renowned evangelist T. L. Osborn notes, "After purging us from our sins, making us worthy to share His life and virtue, *He sat down*. But it is not our time to sit down. It is our time to *stand up!* His redemptive work is *finished*. Now He has committed to us the continuation of His ministry, as His representatives, as His interpreters. He has now delegated us to *go* with the good news, as His ambassadors, and to act on His behalf and in His name."[14]

It is my fervent prayer that this book on heaven will stoke fires for the fulfilling of the Great Commission. May Christ's love compel us to bring other people with us to heaven. It is time to pull out all the stops and give ourselves without reserve for Christ and His global glory. John Piper challenges us, "If we are exiles and refugees on earth (1 Peter 2:11), and if our citizenship is in heaven (Philippians 3:20), and if nothing can separate us from the love of Christ (Romans 8:35), and if his steadfast love is better than life (Psalm 63:3), and if all hardship is working for us an eternal weight of glory (2 Corinthians 4:17), then we will give to the winds our fears and 'seek first the kingdom of God and his righteousness' (Matthew 6:33). We will count everything as rubbish in comparison with Christ (Philippians 3:7–8)."[15]

God help us to see a world in need of Christ. Billy Graham's challenge to thousands of international evangelists gathered in 2000 in Amsterdam is a call to us as well: "Let us light a fire of commitment to proclaim the gospel of Jesus Christ in the power of the Holy Spirit to the ends of the earth, using every resource at our command and with every ounce of our strength."[16]

AN ANCHOR FOR THE SOUL

When heaven matters to us, the gospel will matter to us. When heaven is center stage, the gospel will be center stage. The essence of our message—Christ crucified and risen—will be restored to its rightful place of preeminence. I am sick at heart that it is increasingly possible to slip into many evangelical churches *for weeks* and never hear the gospel. If the pastors of these churches lived as if heaven matters, it would not be so.

During the brutal days of communism, Alexander Solzhenitsyn was confined in the depressing Soviet gulags. He was an "enemy of the state" because he loved freedom and he loved Jesus. With the other prisoners Solzhenitsyn worked in the fields. His tedious days were a cruel pattern of backbreaking work and slow starvation.

Finally one day the hopelessness of the situation overwhelmed him. Solzhenitsyn felt no reason to go on living. His life seemed worthless as he slowly rotted in that unrelenting prison. Solzhenitsyn reached the breaking point. Laying down his shovel, he walked slowly to a crude bench. He knew death was probably only minutes away. Soon a guard would order him back to work, and when he failed to respond, he would probably be bludgeoned to death with his own shovel. He had seen this happen to other fellow prisoners.

As Solzhenitsyn sat waiting, he suddenly felt a presence. Lifting his eyes he saw that an old man was now seated next to him. The old prisoner, without saying a word, drew a stick through the sand at Solzhenitsyn's feet, tracing out the sign of the cross.

Solzhenitsyn stared at the cross, and his entire perspective changed. He knew he was just one broken man pitted against a powerful, dehumanizing Communist machine. But the cross gave him hope. He knew that the hope of all humanity was represented in that cross. Through the power of the cross, all things were possible. Solzhenitsyn slowly got up and went back to work.

History would soon make dramatic, sharp turns. Solzhenitsyn would be miraculously freed. His writings would expose the fallaciousness of the Communist system and identify the fault lines that were about to shift and crumble. Today, the Union of Soviet Socialist Republics has vanished from the face of the earth. And Alexander Solzhenitsyn in his own lifetime has already gone down in history as one of freedom's greatest advocates.[17]

Such is the power of the cross of Jesus Christ. His cross matters. His resurrection matters. Heaven and salvation matter. And it is these verities that anchor us in the midst of the great, final shaking of this planet.

The events of the last few years indicate that we have embarked on the final shaking prophesied in Hebrews. This shaking is so "that the things which cannot be shaken may remain" (Heb. 12:27). It is a time of violent spiritual turbulence as hurricane winds of doubt, hurt, and lost confidence are blasting away at the faith of millions. Seemingly everything we possess, spiritually and emotionally, that's not bolted down is being blown away.

In light of these conditions, how then should we live? After pronouncing this time of shaking, the writer of Hebrews calls us to a distinctive standard of living. "Therefore, since we are receiving a kingdom which cannot be shaken, let us have grace, by which we may serve God acceptably with reverence and godly fear" (Heb. 12:28). Notice that we are not merely to serve God; we are to serve Him in an acceptable fashion. Reverence for God is always the climate that produces acceptable service.

Bruce Wilkinson reminds us, "Serve faithfully here, rule perfectly there.... Don't waste another day living for less. Your commission for Jesus is as big as the world (Mark 16:15). Your opportunity is now. Serve Him faithfully on earth and you will be wonderfully, fully, perfectly prepared to do what you will desperately crave to do in heaven."[18] And what you will crave to do in heaven is lovingly serve your Savior in His never-ending rule over a new heaven and a new earth.

Our acceptable service now is predicated on the bedrock fact that we are headed for an unshakable kingdom. Things (and people) once thought impeccably secure are being ripped from their hinges. The double lives of once-esteemed leaders of the church have been exposed. Many Christians are being "tossed to and fro and carried about with every wind of doctrine" (Eph. 4:14). In a world gone mad, what on earth *abides*?

The essence of our relationship with Christ abides, transcending the erosion of time and the assaults of its enemies. What is this essence? Faith, hope, and love. Make no mistake: the devil has targeted these essential spiritual components. He attacks faith by trying to make us skeptical. He targets love by attempting to make us critical. And he fires at hope by trying to make us cynical. Still, these durable components remain. We bolster faith by God's Word. God's love is poured out in our hearts by the Holy Spirit. And we cultivate hope by living as if heaven matters. "And now abide faith, hope, love..." (1 Cor. 13:13).

The character of God also remains unchanged. He is forever love; He is forever holy.[19] God has entered into a covenant oath of love with you. He has promised never to leave or forsake you.[20] His work in you, as it is with all creation, is permanent and ongoing.[21] And since it is impossible for God to lie, Scripture says we have strong consolation.[22]

Certainly not least in our core of unshakable things is our confidence of heaven and all it holds. The return of Christ is the blessed hope of the believer. And the sure prospect of an eternity with Him keeps us anchored when gale-force winds blow. In the midst of hell's bombardments there is assurance of victory for those "who have fled for refuge to lay hold of the hope set before us. This hope we have as an anchor of the soul, both sure and steadfast" (Heb. 6:18–19).

No greater gift could be given you than the assurance of a sure future, a rock-solid "hope which is laid up for you in heaven" (Col. 1:5). Even your present trials are pregnant with hope because He lives. You have been born again, not to a death wish, but to a living, confident hope.

FOREVER FAITHFUL

Alexander Pope said, "Hope springs eternal in the human breast." But for Christian believers this is not hope in the abstract. Our hope has an object—Jesus Christ. He is our hope. Hope does indeed spring eternal when you live as if heaven matters. This allows us to smile through pain and live steadily through disasters.

Jeremiah had watched his nation be pillaged methodically by ruthless enemies. Yet, in the throes of national defeat and personal anguish he worshiped God, declaring, "His compassions fail not. They are new every morning; great is Your faithfulness. 'The LORD is my portion,' says my soul, 'therefore I hope in Him!'" (Lam. 3:22–24).

The majestic hymn "Now Thank We All Our God" was written by Martin Rinkhart during the Thirty Years' War of 1618–1648 while he was a pastor at Eilenburg in Saxony. The little town was severely attacked three times, yet it served as a haven for refugees. There was intense famine and pestilence. For some time Rinkhart was the only pastor in the city, and during the great pestilence of 1637, he conducted about forty-five hundred burial services—sometimes as many as forty or fifty a day. In the midst of these horrendous circumstances, he wrote these lines of thanksgiving to God:

> Now thank we all our God with hearts and hands and voices,
> Who wondrous things has done, in Whom this world rejoices;
> Who from our mothers' arms has blessed us on our way
> With countless gifts of love, and still is ours today.[23]

Because we see beyond the present to an eternally wonderful future, we stay steady in adversity. Pain is temporary. Heaven's joy is eternal.

Just think of it. The Bible teaches we will "sit down with Abraham, Isaac, and Jacob in the kingdom of heaven" (Matt. 8:11). I believe that right now the saints of previous ages are conversing in heaven—not about their past accomplishments but about the present church's opportunities. A family friend was declared clinically dead for several hours and related that during those hours he was transported to heaven. He described, as best he could, what glorious things he saw there. Of particular interest to me was how he said he saw my father, who was a great missions enthusiast, and David Livingstone engaged in joyful conversation. No doubt, their subject was world evangelization—not in their generations, but in this one.

As we have seen, the church is never diminished by the death of its members. Earthbound believers enjoy a "mystic, sweet communion with those whose race is won." Followers of Jesus who have preceded us to heaven have simply been restationed for a new assignment. Disappointments are for them forever a thing of the past. If you know Jesus, there is an inevitably brighter tomorrow. The church's one foundation now, then, and always is Jesus Christ, her Lord. Even in the midst of our indefensible shortcomings, He will lead His church to ultimate victory.

> 'Mid toil and tribulation and tumult of her war,
> She waits the consummation of peace forevermore;
> Till, with the vision glorious, her longing eyes are blest,
> And the great Church victorious shall be the Church at rest.[24]

Twice in Revelation we are told that God will wipe away all tears.[25] When we get to heaven we will be far more acutely aware of lost time and lost opportunities. For many, the response will be tears of regret. And for all of us there will be, no doubt, one final burst of emotional release that brings total healing. In ministry to the hurting, I've witnessed that just prior to a deep work of inner healing there is often an outburst of crying. Just so, our tears of remorse, regret, and release will be washed away in the sea of His firm, tender love on that day.

You may be in the thick of confusing conflicts, even now. The thermostat of affliction may have been turned up higher. If so, there are three simple assurances you need to recall.

First, *Jesus Christ is going to win*. Every knee will one day bow to Him. Every human, angelic, and demonic tongue will confess, "Jesus Christ is Lord." The present struggles for world domination will have no effect on the final outcome. The battle for this planet is fixed! Jesus shall reign.

Second, *you are going to win*. You have been purchased with the blood of Jesus. He has an enormous vested interest in you. Absolutely nothing in your past, present, or future can sever you from His love. He has taken you on as a lifetime project. And He has vowed to finish in you what He has started.[26]

Third, *the church is going to win*. The present convulsions, attacks, and apparent recessions are temporary. One day Christ's global glory will not be a distant dream; it will be a realized hope. Not only will heaven ring with His praises, "the earth will be filled with the knowledge of the glory of the LORD, as the waters cover the sea" (Hab. 2:14). You are on the winning team.

AT THE FEET OF JESUS

J. H. Thornwell observed, "If the church could be aroused to a deeper sense of the glory that awaits her, she would enter with a warmer spirit into the struggles that are before her."[27] That's what I've attempted to do in these pages—arouse in us as Jesus followers a deeper sense of the glories that await us. Thus strengthened, we are equipped for victory in our present struggles. A greater revelation of our future gives us a clearer perception of our present. A greater revelation of Christ gives us a clearer perception of His amazing grace.

The problem with the things we give so much of our time to is not so much that those things are evil. It's just that, from eternity's perspective, they're worthless. They have no eternal value. Let me be pointed with you. Time is not on your side, or mine. We have one less day to prepare for eternity than we had yesterday. So, let's drop what's worthless and pursue what has lasting value. "Since... you have been raised with Christ, set your hearts on things above, where Christ is seated at the right hand of God. Set your minds on things above, not on earthly things. For you died, and your life is now hidden with Christ in God. When Christ, who is your life, appears, then you also will appear with him in glory" (Col. 3:1–4, NIV). God give us hearts recalibrated toward heaven.

The big deal is pleasing Jesus—here and for eternity. Rick Warren reminds us, "One day you will stand before God, and he will do an audit of your life; a final exam, before you enter eternity.... Fortunately, God wants us to pass this test, so he has given us the questions in advance. From the Bible we can surmise that God will ask us two crucial questions: First, *'What did you do with my Son, Jesus Christ?'* Second, *'What did you do with what I gave you?'*"[28]

We have only begun, C. S. Lewis wrote, the "Great Story which no one on earth has read: which with every chapter is better than the one before."[29] Heaven holds all the secrets that time will never tell. One day God will lovingly give a full disclosure of the *why* behind every pain, disappointment, and heartache. "All that I know now is partial and incomplete, but then I will know everything completely, just as God knows me now" (1 Cor. 13:12, NLT). J. I. Packer observes, "Hearts on earth may say in the course of a joyful experience, 'I don't want this ever to end.' But invariably it does. The hearts of those in heaven say, 'I want this to go on forever.' And it will. There is no better news than this."[30]

I've been privileged to meet some godly giants of the past in the latter years of their lives here on Earth. Each of these men was renowned in his day. Yet each of them lived to an age when the Christian public, though continuing to respect them, bypassed them for younger, more contemporary leaders. I cannot say that I was close to any of these men.

My encounters with them were few and brief, but each of them marked my life. They shared one common trait: they all seemed so conscious of heaven, so in touch with another world.

Heaven's signals are often silenced amid today's clamor. But those who mark their world, as Thoreau reminded us, are those who hear and march to the beat of a different drummer. We are to live for what matters. And what matters here are those very few, highly precious things we can take with us into eternity. We will travel light when we finally go home. Our baggage will consist of people we have brought to Christ and the intimacy with God we've developed.

That's it. That's all the baggage this final flight will allow. You can't take your money with you. But you can transfer Earth's currency and commodities into heaven's tender. You can lay up treasures in heaven by investing in the advance of His kingdom on Earth. You can send a great deal on ahead in preparation for your coming. To give up rusting riches now for timeless treasures then makes sense—if you live as if heaven matters. Jim Elliot was right: "That man is no fool who gives up that which he cannot keep to gain that which he cannot lose." You will never regret living these days in light of that day. And you would sorely regret *not* doing so.

All of us have a long way to go toward Christlikeness. Someone said, "I won't arrive until He arrives." Still, we keep pressing toward the goal of conformity to Him. "I do not count myself to have apprehended; but one thing I do, forgetting those things which are behind and reaching forward to those things which are ahead, I press toward the goal for the prize of the upward call of God in Christ Jesus" (Phil. 3:13–14).

As we run for the prize, the distractions are legion: the weights of life, easily besetting sins, and the taunts and jeers of those already sidelined. The best insurance that you will finish honorably is to stop your ears to the heckling of the critics and the pleadings of your own flesh and fix your eyes, your heart, and your total energies on the goal. As you close this book, open wide your heart. Resolve to live as if heaven matters. For it surely does. And as you prepare for your personal appointment with

Jesus, you can rejoice in His ongoing work of transforming you into His likeness. "If you learn to live in the white light of Christ here and now," Oswald Chambers noted, "judgment finally will cause you to delight in the work of God in you. Keep yourself steadily faced by the judgment seat of Christ."[31]

Everything—that's right, *everything*—will soon find its consummation in Jesus Christ. We will forever be wrapped up in Him. "For God has allowed us to know the secret of his plan, and it is this: he purposed long ago in his sovereign will that all human history shall be consummated in Christ, that everything that exists in Heaven or earth shall find its perfection and fulfillment in him" (Eph. 1:10, PHILLIPS).

Because of Jesus, we are headed for a new heaven and a new earth. "We won't float away on illuminated cotton clouds," David Bryant explains. "Instead, the current creation will be both emancipated and renovated by Jesus for our full use. To our joy themes derived from the initial Garden of Eden will be reactivated, though greatly expanded. Creation, liberated from the bondage of decay, will be incorporated into a new world, concentrated within the jeweled walls of a new city fashioned by the Architect of Heaven (as the colorful imagery of the last two chapters of Revelation details for us)."[32]

So, look up! Your redemption is close at hand.[33] Anchor upward! Live as if heaven matters. God is and forever will be faithful to you. "He will keep you strong to the end, so that you will be blameless on the day of our Lord Jesus Christ. God, who has called you into fellowship with his Son Jesus Christ our Lord, is faithful" (1 Cor. 1:8, NIV).

Andre Crouch's song "Soon and Very Soon," which tells us that soon we are going to see our King, is even timelier now than when he penned it years ago. By God's grace, I'll see you in heaven. And together we will see the King.

Where can you look for me?

I'll be the blood-bought man lying face down in awestruck adoration at His pierced feet.

SCRIPTURE INDEX

Genesis
8:22   *68*
12:1–3   *196*
15:1   *157*
18, 19   *137*

1 Samuel
3:1–21   *201*
30:24   *79*

2 Samuel
24:24   *75, 115*

1 Kings
19:11–12   *200*

2 Kings
6:15–17   *201*

1 Chronicles
11:18   *74*

2 Chronicles
16:9   *79*

Job
19:25–26   *169*

Psalms
30:5   *68*

31:15   *202*
33:1   *200*
40:3   *151*
58:11   *46*
63:3   *172*
75:6–7   *79*
90:12   *49*
116:15   *68*
119:89   *110*
126:5   *130*
126:6   *129*
131:1   *111*
139:24   *149*

Proverbs
4:18   *66*
10:7   *158*
11:18   *46, 110*
14:26   *157*
23:4   *89*
31:11   *25*

Ecclesiastes
3:11   *5*
3:14   *203*

Isaiah
6:3   *202*

40:10   *47*
40:13   *58*
40:29–31   *139–140*
53:5   *60*
53:7   *196*
55:8–9   *58*
65:17   *38*
66:1   *109*
66:8   *129*
66:22   *38*

Jeremiah
18:7–8   *44*

Lamentations
3:22–24   *176*

Daniel
12:3   *113*

Hosea
10:12   *118*

Joel
2:25   *196*

Amos
4:12   *191*

Habakkuk
2:14   *178*

Malachi
3:16   *106*

Matthew
4:4   *155*

5:5   *190, 198*
5:7   *114*
5:10–12   *100*
5:11–12   *47*
5:12   *114*
5:13   *201*
6:1–20   *193*
6:3–4   *47*
6:4   *97*
6:6   *47, 112*
6:10   *37*
6:19–21   *119, 197*
6:20   *48*
6:24   *196*
6:33   *173*
7:13–14   *195*
8:16–17   *53*
8:11   *177*
10:26   *88, 190*
10:41   *113, 130, 198*
10:42   *198*
12:36   *190, 197*
13:17   *28, 150*
16:24–27   *113*
16:27   *47, 123*
18:3   *190*
18:4   *114*
19:21   *197*
24:12   *42*
25:21   *110, 115*
25:26   *26*
28:19   *202*

Mark

4:22   *86*
8:38   *49*
9:23   *157*
9:41   *47*
9:48   *64*
10:42–45   *73*
16:15   *175, 202*
16:15–20   *54*

Luke

6:22–23   *49, 87*
6:35   *47*
9:1–2   *54*
12:15   *42*
12:21   *43*
12:33   *113, 197*
12:42–44   *126*
16:13   *196*
21:25   *44*
21:26   *71, 153*
21:26–28   *200*
21:27–28   *203*
24:47   *202*

John

1:12   *18*
3:1–21   *196*
3:3   *190*
3:16   *77*
3:36   *202*
4:14   *18*
5:22–23   *92*
7:37   *8*

10:27   *155*
11:26   *59*
12:26   *145*
14:1–3   *29*
14:2–3   *167*
14:19   *60, 169*
17:3   *23*
19:30   *172*
20:21   *202*

Acts

1:8   *202*
2:18–21   *198*
15:14   *172*
17:30–31   *121*
17:31   *167*

Romans

1:17   *103*
2:16   *83*
3:19   *139*
3:23   *195*
5:12   *195*
8:15   *105*
8:23   *60*
8:28–29   *143*
8:35   *172*
12:12   *166*
12:19   *6*
14:8   *66*
14:10   *196*
14:10–13   *123*
15:9   *172*

15:13   *168*
15:16   *202*

1 Corinthians
1:8   *181*
2:9   *34, 133*
3:11–15   *136*
4:3   *122*
4:5   *106, 144*
9:25, 27   *129*
13:12   *179*
13:13   *175*
15:19   *10*
15:52   *59*
15:54–57   *71*

2 Corinthians
2:16   *85*
3:18   *143*
4:16   *60*
4:17   *172*
4:17–18   *10*
5:1–2   *12*
5:3–4   *11*
5:6, 8   *194*
5:6–8   *24*
5:6–9   *61*
5:9   *13, 143*
5:9–10   *199*
5:9–11   *94*
5:10   *41, 196*
5:11   *104*
5:14   *8*
12:8–10   *56*

Galatians
6:7–9   *118*
6:10   *196*

Ephesians
1:10   *181*
1:18   *166*
2:7   *15*
2:8–10   *137*
2:12–14   *164*
4:14   *175*
5:15–16   *50*
6:6–8   *113*
6:11–18   *199*

Philippians
1:6   *144, 203*
1:21   *24*
1:21, 23   *194*
1:23   *11*
2:5   *74*
2:9–11   *76*
2:16   *144*
2:17   *76*
3:7–8   *173*
3:13–14   *51, 180*
3:19–20   *149*
3:20   *172, 190*
3:20–21   *41*
3:21   *167*
4:1   *149*

Colossians
1:5   *176*
1:3–5   *166*

1:16–18 *170*
1:27 *168*
3:1–2 *15*
3:1–4 *179*
3:23–24 *47*

1 Thessalonians
2:19–20 *130, 157*
4:15–17 *65*
4:16–17 *167*
5:23 *199*

2 Thessalonians
1:7–9 *22*
1:7–10 *124*

1 Timothy
1:1 *166*
4:8 *112*
5:24–25 *106*
6:19 *48, 197*

2 Timothy
1:12 *106*
2:12 *116*
2:21 *114*
3:2–5 *75*
3:12 *99*
4:5 *129*
4:6–7 *70*
4:7–8 *125*
4:8 *123*

Titus
1:1–2 *166*

2:11–13 *84*
2:13 *166, 198*
3:5 *112*

Hebrews
1:3 *202*
2:9 *66*
2:10 *117*
4:12 *114*
6:18 *202*
6:18–19 *176*
7:25 *105*
9:27 *62*
10:23 *135*
10:32–35 *48*
11:6 *112, 115, 201*
11:8–10 *147*
11:10 *38, 148*
11:13–16 *80*
11:24–26 *109*
11:26 *100, 117*
11:27 *154*
11:35 *117*
11:35–37 *106*
11:38 *99*
12:1 *198*
12:1–2 *120*
12:1–3 *99*
12:2 *117*
12:14–15 *142*
12:27 *174*
12:27–29 *156*
12:28 *174*
12:28–29 *13*

13:3   *100*
13:5   *202*
13:14   *36*

James
1:12   *128*
2:9   *197*
3:1   *85*
4:6, 10   *195*
4:14   *189, 200*

1 Peter
1:3–4   *163, 199*
1:6–7   *145*
1:15   *103*
2:9   *28*
2:11   *172*
2:21–23   *98*
3:22   *81*
4:9   *198*
4:12–13   *114*
4:14   *145*
4:17   *85*
5:1–4   *131*
5:5–6   *118, 195*

2 Peter
1:10–11   *19*
1:11   *20, 24*
2:15   *190*
3:10   *121*

1 John
1:5   *31*
2:15   *42, 191*

2:16   *198*
2:28   *25, 49*
3:2   *144*
3:2–3   *166*
3:3   *125*
4:8   *202*
4:19   *111*

2 John
8   *48, 139*

Jude
24   *3, 143*

Revelation
1:10   *123*
1:14–17   *123*
2, 3   *155*
2:7   *200*
2:10   *49, 127*
2:26–28   *197*
3:11   *138*
7:17; 21:4   *203*
11:15   *132, 167*
14:13   *159, 197*
19:12, 16   *198*
20:11–15   *199*
21:1   *38, 167*
21:1–5   *xi*
21:4   *38*
21:9–22   *192*
21:23; 22:5   *31*
21:27   *197*
22:12   *48*
22:17   *101*

NOTES

INTRODUCTION

1. Stuart McAllister, "Permanent Things" (message delivered at conference on "Permanent Things," Winter 2001). Reference provided by Ravi Zacharias International Ministries, http://rzim.org/resources/jttran.php?seqid=75 (accessed April 27, 2007).

2. Dietrich Bonhoeffer, *Ethics*, translated by Neville Horton Smith (New York: Touchstone, 1995), 78.

3. C. S. Lewis, *The Joyful Christian* (New York: Touchstone, 1996), 138.

CHAPTER ONE
ANCHORED UPWARD

1. Philip Yancey, *Rumors of Another World* (Grand Rapids, MI: Zondervan, 2003), 120.

2. James 4:14.

3. Judson Cornwall, *Things You Don't Know About Heaven* (Lake Mary, FL: Charisma House, 2007), 11.

4. Charles F. Kettering, quoted on the Kettering Fund Web site, http://www.ketteringfund.org/related.html (accessed April 30, 2007).

5. E. M. Bounds, *Catching a Glimpse of Heaven* (Springdale, PA: Whitaker House, 1985), 98.

6. "Must I Go, and Empty-Handed?" by Charles C. Luther. Public domain.

7. Alexander Solzhenitsyn, *Gulag Archipelago II* (New York: Harper & Row, 1975), 615.

8. Quoted in Randy Alcorn, *Heaven* (Carol Stream, IL: Tyndale House Publishers, 2004), 207.

9. Philippians 3:20.

10. Mark Twain, *The Adventures of Huckleberry Finn* (Cheswold, DE: Prestwick House, 2005), 14 (originally published 1899 by Harper & Brothers, New York).

11. Matthew 5:5.

12. A. W. Tozer, *The Pursuit of God* (Harrisburg, PA: Christian Publications, 1982), 113.

13. "The Solid Rock" by Edward Mote. Public domain.

14. Quoted in Alcorn, *Heaven*, 95.

15. Joseph M. Stowell, *Eternity* (Chicago, Moody Press, 1995), 27.

16. Matthew 12:36.

17. Matthew 10:26.

18. Matthew 18:3.

19. John 3:3.

CHAPTER TWO

A RICH WELCOME

1. D. L. Moody, "Its Happiness," *Heaven* (1908). Reference provided by Memorial University of Newfoundland, http://www.mun.ca/rels/restmov/texts/dasc/HVN03.HTM (accessed April 19, 2007).

2. 2 Peter 2:15.

3. Shakespeare, *As You Like It*, 2.7. Reference provided by Massachusetts Institute of Technology, "The Complete Works of William Shakespeare," http://shakespeare.mit.edu/asyoulikeit/asyoulikeit.2.7.html (accessed May 1, 2007). References are to act and scene.

4. Philip Yancey, "Heaven Can't Wait," *Christianity Today*, September 7, 1984, 53.

5. Amos 4:12.

6. *The Martyrdom of Polycarp* 11.2, revised into modern English by Richard Neil Shrout, from the translation of J. B. Lightfoot. Reference provided by the Early Christian Writings Web site, http://ministries.tliquest.net/theology/apocryphas/nt/martyr.htm (accessed May 1, 2007).

7. Center for Reformed Theology and Apologetics (CRTA), "Westminster Confession of Faith 33," http://www.reformed.org/documents/wcf_with_proofs/ (accessed April 23, 2007).

8. Southern Baptist Convention, "The Baptist Faith and Message 10," http://www.sbc.net/bfm/bfm2000.asp#ii (accessed April 23, 2007).

9. General Council of the Assemblies of God, "Assemblies of God Statement of Fundamental Truths 15," http://ag.org/top/Beliefs/Statement_of_Fundamental_Truths/sft_full.cfm#15 (accessed April 23, 2007).

10. John Fischer, "People Get Ready," *Contemporary Christian Music*, September 1996, 84.

11. 1 John 2:15.

12. Oswald Chambers, *My Utmost for His Highest* (Uhrichsville, OH: Barbour Publishing, n.d.), 233.

13. James Hudson Taylor, *A Retrospective by Hudson Taylor* (Chicago: Moody Press, 1950), 19.

14. Quoted by Malcolm Muggeridge, *A Twentieth Century Testimony* (Nashville, TN: Thomas Nelson Publishers, 1978), 16.

CHAPTER THREE
YOU CAN ONLY IMAGINE

1. Jonathan Edwards, *The Christian Pilgrim* (1733). Reference provided by Bible Bulletin Board, http://www.biblebb.com/FILES/EDWARDS/PILGRIM.HTM (accessed April 23, 2007).

2. Ken Gire, *Windows of the Soul* (Grand Rapids, MI: Zondervan, 1996), 84.

3. Choo Thomas, *Heaven Is So Real!* (Lake Mary, FL: Charisma House, 2003), 41.

4. Don Piper, *90 Minutes in Heaven* (Grand Rapids, MI: Fleming H. Revell, 2004), 24–25.

5. Ibid.

6. Revelation 21:9–22. I have relied heavily on the research of Judson Cornwall in this area, particularly from chapter 5 of his book *Things You Don't Know About Heaven*.

7. "I Can Only Imagine" by Bart Millard. Copyright © 2001, 2002 Simpleville Music (admin by Simpleville Music, Inc.). All rights reserved. International copyright secured. Used by permission.

8. Lewis, *The Joyful Christian*, 228.

9. Aldous Huxley, *Brave New World* (New York: HarperCollins, 1932).

10. Joseph Bayle, "What Heaven Will Be Like," *Moody Monthly*, May 1976, 27.

11. Paul Billheimer, *Destined for the Throne* (Fort Washington, PA: Christian Literature Crusade, 1975).

12. Reggie McNeal, *Practicing Greatness* (San Francisco, CA: Jossey-Bass, 2006), 72.

13. C. S. Lewis, *Mere Christianity* (New York: Macmillan, 1943), 118.

14. Calvin Miller, lecture at Southwestern Baptist Theological Seminary, 1978.

15. St. Augustine, *City of God* (New York: Doubleday, 1979).

16. Quoted in Alcorn, *Heaven*, 99.

17. Jack W. Hayford, general editor, *Hayford's Bible Handbook* (Nashville, TN: Thomas Nelson, 1995), 636.

18. Wayne Gruden, *Systematic Theology: An Introduction to Biblical Doctrines* (Grand Rapids, MI: Zondervan, 1994), 1158.

19. Edith Schaeffer, "Illusion or Reality?" *Christianity Today*, March 12, 1976.

20. C. S. Lewis, *The Problem of Pain* (Glasgow: William Collins Sons & Co., Ltd., 1940), 115.

21. "When We All Get to Heaven" by Eliza Hewitt. Public domain.

CHAPTER FOUR

HEAVEN: THE SAFEST
INVESTMENT ON EARTH

1. Lewis, *The Problem of Pain*, 115.

2. William James, *The Letters of William James* (1920) (Whitefish, MT: Kessinger Publishing, 2003), 260.

3. Philip Yancey, *Rumors of Another World* (Grand Rapids, MI: Zondervan, 2003), 201.

4. CreativeQuotations.com, "Creative Quotations From Henry Ward Beecher (1813–1887)," http://creativequotations.com/one/61s024.htm (accessed May 3, 2007).

5. Jonathan Edwards, *The Works of Jonathan Edwards*, vol. 1 (1834). Reference provided by Christian Classics Ethereal Library (CCEL), http://www.ccel.org/ccel/edwards/works1.all.html (accessed May 3, 2007).

6. Rick Howard and Jamie Lash, *This Was Your Life!* (Grand Rapids, MI: Chosen Books, 1998), 52.

7. See Matthew 6:1–20.

8. Howard and Lash, *This Was Your Life!* 52.

9. Bruce Wilkinson, *A Life God Rewards* (Sisters, OR: Multnomah Publishers, 2002), 114.

10. Betty Lee Skinner, *Daws: The Story of Dawson Trotman* (Grand Rapids, MI: Zondervan, 1974), 190, 350.

11. *Hamlet*, 1.3. Reference provided by Massachusettes Institute of Technology, "The Complete Works of William Shakespeare," http://shakespeare.mit.edu/hamlet/hamlet.1.3.html (accessed May 3, 2007). References are to act and scene.

CHAPTER FIVE
BY HIS WOUNDS

1. "There Is a Land of Pure Delight" by Isaac Watts. Public domain.

CHAPTER SIX
DEATH'S DEMISE

1. The Westminster Confession of Faith 32.1–2. Reference provided by the Center for Reformed Theology and Apologetics (CRTA), http://www.reformed.org/documents/westminster_conf_of_faith.html (accessed May 3, 2007).

2. John Milton, *Paradise Lost* 1.61–67. Reference provided by Dartmouth College, http://www.dartmouth.edu/~milton/reading_room/pl/book_1/index.shtml (accessed May 3, 2007). References are to book and lines.

3. 2 Corinthians 5:6, 8; Philippians 1:21, 23.

4. Robert J. Morgan, *On This Day* (Nashville: Thomas Nelson, 1997), 27.

5. David Watson, *Fear No Evil* (London: Hodder & Stoughton, 1984), 164.

6. Erwin Lutzer, *One Minute After You Die* (Chicago, IL: Moody Publishers, 1997), 96.

7. "It Is Well With My Soul" by Horatio G. Spafford. Public domain.

8. Herbert Lockyer, *Last Words of Saints and Sinners* (Grand Rapids, MI: Kregel Publications, 1969), 114.

CHAPTER SEVEN

THE CHEMISTRY OF THE UNIVERSE

1. Andrew Murray, *Humility* (Gainesville, FL: Bridge-Logos Publishers, 2000), 94.

2. Quoted in Harold Myra and Marshall Shelly, *The Leadership Secrets of Billy Graham* (Grand Rapids, MI: Zondervan, 2005), 198.

3. James 4:6, 10; 1 Peter 5:5–6.

4. "Jesus Loves the Little Children" by George F. Root. Public domain.

5. Yancey, *Rumors of Another World*, 60–61.

6. Richard Foster, *Celebration of Discipline* (San Francisco: HarperSanFrancisco, 1978, 1988, 1998), 130.

7. Quoted in Wilkinson, *A Life God Rewards*, 119–120.

8. Murray, *Humility*, ix.

9. Dietrich Bonhoeffer, *The Cost of Discipleship* (New York: The Macmillan Company, 1970), 211.

10. Matthew 7:13–14.

11. Paul Rees, quoted in *Encyclopedia of 7700 Illustrations* (Rockville, MD: Assurance Publishers, 1979), 1371–1372.

CHAPTER EIGHT

IS THAT YOUR FINAL ANSWER?

1. Romans 3:23; 5:12.

2. "A Charge to Keep I Have" by Charles Wesley. Public domain.

3. "Come, Thou Fount of Every Blessing" by Robert Robinson. Public domain.

4. Corrie ten Boom, *The Hiding Place* (New York: Bantam Books, 1971), viii.

5. Elisabeth Elliot, *Passion and Purity* (Old Tappan, NJ: Fleming H. Revell Co., 1984), 129–130.

6. Genesis 12:1–3.

7. Matthew 6:24; Luke 16:13.

8. Jerry Cook, *Love, Acceptance and Forgiveness* (Glendale, CA: Regal Books, 1979), 125.

9. Ibid., 125.

10. Stephen R. Covey, *The Seven Habits of Highly Effective People* (New York: Simon and Schuster, 1989), 146–182.

11. R. T. Kendall, *The Anointing: Yesterday, Today, Tomorrow* (Lake Mary, FL: Charisma House, 2003), 160.

12. Galatians 6:10.

13. Wilkinson, *A Life God Rewards*, 65.

14. Kendall, *The Anointing: Yesterday, Today, Tomorrow*, 27.

15. Joel 2:25.

CHAPTER NINE
VINDICATED AT LAST

1. *Richard II*, 3.2. Reference provided by Massachusetts Institute of Technology, "The Complete Works of William Shakespeare," http:// shakespeare.mit.edu/richardii/richardii.3.2.html (accessed May 4, 2007). References are to act and scene.

2. Amy Carmichael, "Hast Thou No Scar?" from the book *Mountain Breezes: The Collected Poems of Amy Carmichael* (Fort Washington, PA: CLC Publications, 1999). Used by permission.

3. Isaiah 53:7.

4. John 3:1–21.

5. Romans 14:10; 2 Corinthians 5:10.

6. Revelation 21:27.

7. Rick Howard, *The Judgment Seat of Christ* (Woodside, CA: Naioth Sound and Publishing, 1990), 36.

8. Quoted by Michael L. Brown, *Revolution!* (Ventura, CA: Renew Books, 2000), 166.

9. Ted Dekker, *The Slumber of Christianity* (Nashville, TN: Nelson Books, 2005), 74.

10. George Barna, *The Second Coming of the Church* (Nashville, TN: Word Publishing, 1998), 120–121.

11. "The Great Assize," preached on March 10, 1758. John Wesley, *The Works of the Rev. John Wesley: Sermons, Vol. 1* (New York: Hunt and Eaton, 1825), 27.

12. James 2:9.

13. W. E. Vine, *Vine's Expository Dictionary of New Testament Words* (Peabody, MA: Hendrickson Publishers, 1989), 414.

14. Matthew 12:36.

15. Revelation 14:13.

16. Matthew 6:19–21; 19:21; Luke 12:33; 19:17, 19; 1 Timothy 6:19; Revelation 2:26–28.

CHAPTER TEN

A SURE REWARD

1. Stuart McAllister, "Permanent Things" (message delivered at conference on "Permanent Things," Winter 2001). Reference provided by Ravi Zacharias International Ministries, http://rzim.org/resources/jttran.php?seqid=75 (accessed May 7, 2007).

2. John Bevere, *Driven by Eternity* (New York: Warner Faith, 2006), 189.

3. Of course, I am not implying that we should indenture ourselves as slaves to companies or employers. The thought is that we are to be conscientious stewards, doing our work ultimately as to the Lord.

4. Matthew 10:41; 1 Peter 4:9.

5. Bevere, *Driven by Eternity*, 190.

6. J. I. Packer, *Knowing God* (Downers Grove, IL: InterVarsity, 1973), 76.

7. "Am I a Soldier of the Cross?" by Isaac Watts. Public domain.

8. Murray, *Humility*, 2.

9. Matthew 5:5.

CHAPTER ELEVEN
TREASURES IN HEAVEN

1. 1 John 2:16.

2. Karl Marx, "Introduction (1844)," *Critique of Hegel's Philosophy of Right* (1843–1844), trans. Annette Jolin and Joseph O'Malley (Cambridge, UK: Cambridge University Press, 1970). Reference provided by http://www.marxists.org/archive/marx/works/1843/critique-hpr/intro.htm (accessed May 8, 2007).

3. Acts 2:18–21, KJV.

4. Matthew 10:42.

5. Vine, *Vine's Expository Dictionary of New Testament Words*, 250. See Revelation 19:12, 16.

6. Kendall, *The Anointing: Yesterday, Today, Tomorrow*, 47.

7. Titus 2:13.

8. Hebrews 12:1.

9. Philip Yancey, "Why Not Now?" *Christianity Today*, February 5, 1996, 112.

10. EnglishMonarchs.co, "The Crown Jewels," http://www
    .englishmonarchs.co.uk/crown_jewels.htm (accessed May 8, 2007).

11. "The Day Thou Gavest, Lord, Is Ended" by John Ellerton. Public
    domain.

CHAPTER TWELVE

BUILT TO LAST

1. "Battle Hymn of the Republic" by Julia Ward Howe. Public domain.

2. 2 Corinthians 5:9–10; Revelation 20:11–15.

3. Howard and Lash, *This Was Your Life*, 65.

4. Ephesians 6:11–18.

5. Quoted in John Piper, *Desiring God* (Sisters, OR: Multnomah
   Publishers, 2003), 142.

6. Arthur T. Pierson, *George Müller of Bristol and His Witness to a
   Prayer-Hearing God*, "At Evening-Time—Light" (Old Tappan, NJ:
   Fleming H. Revell Company, 1899), as viewed at BibleBelievers
   .com, http://www.biblebelievers.com/george_muller/g-m_ch19.html
   (accessed May 23, 2007).

7. Neil Postman, "Amusing Ourselves to Death," *Et Cetera*, Spring
   1985, 18.

8. Os Guinness, *Prophetic Untimeliness* (Grand Rapids, MI: Baker
   Books, 2003), 117.

9. Dwight Carlson, *Run and Not Be Weary* (Old Tappan, NJ: Fleming
   H. Revell Company, 1974), 84.

10. Quoted in Dick Eastman, *The Hour That Changes the World* (Grand
    Rapids, MI: Baker Books, 1978), 48.

11. 1 Thessalonians 5:23.

12. 1 Peter 1:3–4.

13. Bud Greenspan, *The 100 Greatest Moments in Sports*, quoted in John C. Maxwell, *The Success Journey* (Nashville, TN: Thomas Nelson Publishers, 1997), 156.

CHAPTER THIRTEEN
SEEING THE INVISIBLE

1. Quoted in Yancey, *Rumors of Another World*, 227.

2. James 4:14.

3. Ann Graham Lotz, *The Vision of His Glory* (Nashville, TN: Word Publishing, 1997), 130–131.

4. Thomas Gray, "Elegy Written in a Country Churchyard," line 73, *The Thomas Gray Archive*, ed. Alexander Huber (Oxford, UK: University of Oxford); reference provided by http://www.thomasgray .org/cgi-bin/display.cgi?text=elcc (accessed May 9, 2007).

5. 1 Kings 19:11–12.

6. Billy Graham Center Archives, "Evangelistic Prayer: The Ministry of Pearl Goode," http://www.wheaton.edu/bgc/archives/docs/goode.htm (accessed May 9, 2007).

7. Billheimer, *Destined for the Throne*, 15.

8. C. S. Lewis, "January 4," *The Business of Heaven: Daily Readings From C. S. Lewis* (New York: Harcourt Trade Publishers, 1984), 19.

9. Psalm 33:1.

10. Wilkinson, *A Life God Rewards*, 62–63.

11. Elizabeth Barrett Browning, *Aurora Leigh*, Oxford World Classics edition, ed. Kerry McSweeney (Oxford, UK: Oxford University Press, 1993), lines 821–824.

12. 2 Kings 6:15–17.

13. Luke 21:26–28.

14. Revelation 2:7.

15. 1 Samuel 3:1–21.

16. James I. Robertson Jr., ed., *Stonewall Jackson's Book of Maxims* (Nashville, TN: Cumberland House Publishers, 2002), 116.

17. Hebrews 11:6.

18. Leonard Ravenhill, *America Is Too Young to Die* (Minneapolis, MN: Bethany Fellowship, 1979), 112.

19. Matthew 5:13.

20. E. M. Bounds, *Power Through Prayer* (Chicago: Moody Press, n.d.), 94.

21. Mother Teresa, *Words to Live By* (New York: Walker Books, 1984), 77.

22. J. Evan Smith, *Booth the Beloved* (Oxford, UK: Oxford University Press, 1949), 123–124, quoted at International Heritage Centre, The Salvation Army, "While Women Weep—I'll Fight," http://www1 .salvationarmy.org/heritage.nsf/0/cdc6918c833e9a3d802568cc00539b 8f?OpenDocument (accessed May 10, 2007).

23. William Carey, *An Enquiry into the obligations of Christians to use means for the conversion of the heathens* (Leicester, England: Henderson & Spalding, 1934 [orig. 1792]), 86–87.

24. Bill Bright, *The Journey Home* (Nashville, TN: Thomas Nelson Publishers, 2003), 3.

25. Ibid., 22.

CHAPTER FOURTEEN

A Theology of Hope

1. "If I Stand" by Rich Mullins. Copyright © 1988 BMG Songs, Inc. (admin by BMG Music Publishing). All rights reserved. Used by permission.

2. Cook, *Love, Acceptance and Forgiveness*, 63.

3. Dekker, *The Slumber of Christianity*, 11.

4. Psalm 31:15.

5. Hayford, gen. ed., *Hayford's Bible Handbook*, 647.

6. "Blessed Assurance" by Fanny J. Crosby. Public domain.

7. The Book of Ruth beautifully illustrates this aspect of Christ's redeeming love for us. By becoming a man, while retaining His full deity, Jesus became both a kinsman and a redeemer to us.

8. David Bryant, *Christ Is All!* (New Providence, NJ: New Providence Publishers, 2004), 27.

9. John 3:36.

10. John Piper, *Don't Waste Your Life* (Wheaton, IL: Crossway Books, 2003), 38.

11. Matthew 28:19; Mark 16:15; Luke 24:47; John 20:21; Acts 1:8.

12. Romans 15:16.

13. Hebrews 1:3.

14. T. L. Osborn, *Soulwinning* (Tulsa, OK: OSFO Publishers, 2000), 33.

15. Piper, *Don't Waste Your Life*, 108.

16. Quoted in David Shibley, *The Missions Addiction* (Lake Mary, FL: Charisma House, 2001), 204.

17. This story is recounted in Charles Colson, *Loving God* (Grand Rapids, MI: Zondervan Publishing House, 1987), 172.

18. Wilkinson, *A Life God Rewards,* 74–75.

19. Isaiah 6:3; 1 John 4:8.

20. Hebrews 13:5.

21. Ecclesiastes 3:14.

22. Hebrews 6:18.

23. "Now Thank We All Our God" by Martin Rinkhart. Public domain.

24. "The Church's One Foundation" by Samuel J. Stone. Public domain.

25. Revelation 7:17; 21:4.

26. Philippians 1:6.

27. James H. Thornwell, *Collected Writings*, vol. 2, p. 48 (1871), as cited by J. Marcellus Kik in *An Eschatology of Victory* (Phillipsburg, NJ: Presbyterian and Reformed Publishing Company, 1971), 6. Reference viewed at Joseph Morecraft III, "Strategy for Invasion and Conquest: Biblical Principles for Christian Political Action in the New Millenium," *The Christian Statesman*, http://www.natreformassn.org/statesman/99/invaconq.html (accessed May 10, 2007).

28. Rick Warren, *The Purpose-Driven Life* (Grand Rapids, MI: Zondervan Publishing House, 2002), 34.

29. C. S. Lewis, *The Last Battle* (New York: HarperCollins, 1994), 211.

30. Quoted in Alcorn, *Heaven*, 198.

31. Chambers, *My Utmost for His Highest*, 53.

32. Bryant, *Christ Is All!* 91.

33. Luke 21:27–28.

Train Leaders. Change Nations.

On the front lines of the church's advance around the world stand God's hidden heroes—national church and marketplace leaders who willingly sacrifice everything to preach the gospel and plant churches among the unreached. Often these church and business leaders in underserved nations face hostile opposition because of their love for Jesus Christ.

David Shibley founded Global Advance to meet the desperate need to equip these leaders to transform their nations. Global Advance equips thousands of men and women every year through Frontline Shepherds Conferences for pastoral leaders and Marketplace Missions Conferences for business leaders. These leaders are equipped to advance the gospel throughout their nations and to surrounding unreached peoples. They receive effective training, relevant resources, and much-needed encouragement. For many it is the only training they have ever received. They go back into the spiritual battle with a vision in their hearts and tools in their hands.

Since 1990 Global Advance has provided on-site training for hundreds of thousands of leaders in more than seventy nations. You are invited to embrace the vision of equipping one million leaders and empowering them to plant one million new churches worldwide. Your prayers and financial support will make a world of difference in the lives of heaven's hidden heroes.

To receive your free subscription to the *Global Advance Update* and David Shibley's *Missions Minute* by e-mail, or for more information about Global Advance's ministry to the church's hidden heroes, contact:

GLOBAL ADVANCE
P. O. Box 742077
Dallas, TX 75374-2077
Phone: (800) 259-9042
Web site: www.globaladvance.org

 GLOBAL ADVANCE

David Shibley is the president and founder of Global Advance, a ministry committed to equipping leaders for evangelism and world harvest.

If you have enjoyed *Living as if Heaven Matters*, you'll love these books on missions and world evangelism.

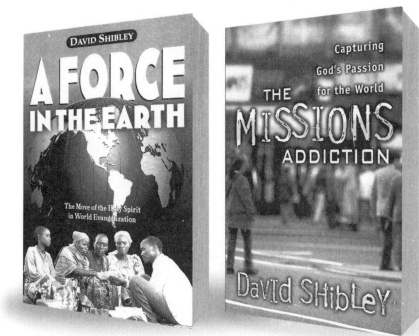

A Force In the Earth

If you are ready to give your all for God, this is a book you have been waiting for! This biblical, informative, and motivational book is an excellence resource for those interested and passionate about evangelizing the world through missions.

978-0-88419-476-7 / $9.99

The Missions Addiction

This is a radical call to mission-minded young adults! God is producing a new force of millennial missionaries who are speaking out in school hallways, college campuses, and in the break rooms at their jobs—and who are making an impact.

978-0-88419-772-0 / $13.99

Visit your local bookstore!

Charisma
HOUSE
A STRANG COMPANY